"*Finding My Vocation* by Pas[tor] young people are questioni[ng] to find their niche in life. This book ma[kes] ple without being shallow, Boekestein examines the biblical concept of vocation as well as how to prepare and practice one's vocation. The content of each chapter is illustrated by the stories of people who were interviewed over the course of writing the book. *Finding My Vocation: A Guide for Young People Seeking a Calling* will be a birthday gift for all my grandchildren who are trying to find their calling. I could not make a better recommendation than that."

Tedd Tripp, pastor emeritus, conference speaker,
author of *Shepherding a Child's Heart*

"Pastor Bill Boekestein has done young people—and the whole church, really—a tremendous service by providing an accessible overview of the Bible's teaching on vocation. We are most happy, and God most glorified, when we live in a manner worthy of the calling to which we have been called. This book will help you do just that. I commend it highly."

Jonathan Landry Cruse, pastor,
Community Presbyterian Church, Kalamazoo, MI

"Pastor Boekestein has written a book that is all at once practical, motivating, challenging, and encouraging. The normal feel-good platitudes of the day won't cut it, and Bill dives into a scriptural take on one of the most important issues and considerations we will ever face. His communication style is clear and succinct, yet with true depth and richness that makes the key takeaways of the book really stick. I cannot recommend this enough!"

David Bahnsen, author of *Full-Time:
Work and the Meaning of Life*

"Thoroughly Reformed. [Boekestein] includes good quotes from the Reformed fathers, confessions, and Scripture."

Garry Eriks, pastor, Unity Protestant Reformed Church,
Byron Center, MI

"Young people seeking God's will for their life's calling will discover a treasure trove of wisdom in William Boekestein's *Finding My Vocation*. Vocation covers all of life. As they prayerfully make decisions for the future, they will consider biblical principles of work and relationships, they will assess their God-given talents and providential circumstances, they will aim to serve their family and their neighbor, and they will honor God. A rich, fulfilling, Christ-centered life awaits them if they follow the principles found on these pages."

Mary Beeke, wife of Joel Beeke and author of *Teach Them to Work: Building a Positive Work Ethic in Our Children*

"This book is packed with biblical truth and practical wisdom— and is a much-needed and extremely helpful resource on the topic of a distinctly Christian view of vocation. I've been helped by it... and I commend it to you."

Jon Nielson, Senior Pastor, Christ Presbyterian Church of Wheaton

"Three things are most important in life: knowing God, marrying the right person, and finding the right vocation. William Boekestein's thoughtful book may help young people follow a good path and recalibrate if they've gone astray."

Marvin Olasky, chairman, Zenger House, and former editor of *WORLD* magazine

"In this book William Boekestein shows us a true pastoral heart. He lays out biblical principles that can enable young readers to seek a vocation that fits them and then do it with gracefulness and God-glorifying purpose. As a founding chancellor of a Christian university in Africa, I will want to put this book into the hands of all our students. The truths in this book could have far-reaching results on our continent!"

Conrad Mbewe, pastor of Kabwata Baptist Church and founding chancellor of the African Christian University in Lusaka, Zambia

"God brings us to our vocations, but his callings still require our preparation and discernment. William Boekestein has written an engaging, biblically and theologically informed guide for young people trying to figure out where God wants them to serve that is both practical and spiritual. But it is also a guide for those of us already deep in our vocations who perhaps do not fully realize the role vocations play in the Christian life."

Gene Edward Veith, emeritus professor of literature, Patrick Henry College, and author of *God at Work: Your Christian Vocation in All of Life*

"I am often asked by worried parents if their teenager should go to college or not. They often mistake an apathy toward higher education as depression, a lack of drive, or just pure laziness. I wonder if in most cases it is a lack of purpose. Many of these parents have fallen into the trap of thinking that a college education is the only avenue to a respectable life. It's simply not true. I value a liberal arts education, and hopefully the children of these worried parents received one in high school. This does not mean, however, that only a white-collar occupation can provide true purpose. Nonsense! Our value, identity, and purpose cannot be satisfactorily defined by salary, position, or social standing. The doctrine of vocation frees us from this false choice. We are first freed from sin on account of Christ. Now that we are free, God uses us, no, he *calls* us to be his coworkers in the world. What title or amount of money could satisfy our yearning for purpose more than that? This book needed to be written. This is tough stuff, isn't it? Especially for teenagers trying to figure out what to do with their lives. Boekestein will help these young Christians navigate these tough questions. He puts the gospel first and by doing so frees the worried teen about their standing before God, but he also shows them that whatever their vocation, it is honored by God. God gives them a divine purpose in life."

Michael Berg, author of *Vocation: The Setting for Human Flourishing*

"Hardly a week goes by when I am not asked an earnest and serious question about vocation. Often it has to do with preparation for work; sometimes it has to do with enduring a job that seems unfulfilling. This short book offers clear, practical, but most importantly, biblical advice on the nature of work, its place in the Christian's life, and how to engage in what God gives us to do. I recommend it highly."

Jonathan Master, president,
Greenville Presbyterian Theological Seminary

"Very thought provoking and practical and...helpful for teens."

Martyn McGeown, pastor, Providence Protestant
Reformed Church, Hudsonville, MI

"Many people spend more of their lives working than any other activity. This wise book blends the insights of several Reformed confessions, the Puritans, and many contemporary voices to create a valuable guide for young people and their parents on vocation. Boekestein is to be commended for this biblical, wise, and highly practical treatment on calling and service to God and our neighbor."

Tom Schwanda, associate professor of Christian formation
and ministry, emeritus, Wheaton College

"Mastering his usual literary skills, William Boekestein covers every aspect of the doctrine of vocation particularly as it applies to young people thinking about their future. Accompanied by true-life examples, this helpful guide is especially timely in a society characterized by a contrasting mixture of high expectations and common anxieties. Even someone like me who has left youthful days far behind can benefit from this reminder and these practical suggestions on how to "lead the life that the Lord has assigned to him, and to which God has called him" (1 Cor. 7:17 ESV). Because of the abundance of scriptural references and pertinent quotations, I have found this book more devotional and nourishing than I would have expected. Highly recommended for the whole family."

Simonetta Carr, mother of eight and author of the
Christian Biographies for Young Readers series

FINDING
MY
VOCATION

FINDING MY VOCATION

A GUIDE FOR YOUNG PEOPLE SEEKING A CALLING

WILLIAM BOEKESTEIN

REFORMED
FREE PUBLISHING
ASSOCIATION

Reformed Free Publishing
1894 Georgetown Center Drive
Jenison, MI 49428
www.rfpa.org
mail@rfpa.org

Author photo: Anya Marie / unscriptedphotographers.com/anyamarie
Cover design: Christopher Tobias / tobiasdesign.com
Interior design: Katherine Lloyd / theDESKonline.com

ISBN: 978-1-959515-29-6
Ebook ISBN: 978-1-959515-30-2
LCCN: 2024940088

To Ron,
for giving me a job,
a place to live,
and so much more
when I desperately needed it

CONTENTS

INTRODUCTION

When we are very young, we enjoy being asked what we want to do when we grow up. And our answers are often creative and well paired with our passions: I want to be an artist, an athlete, or an animal groomer. When young our ambitions have not yet met obstacles. We imagine that we will surely end up doing something we love.

In our teen years and beyond, answering questions about our future is harder. Our interests can change rapidly. We might begin to doubt our abilities. The reality begins to sink in: my future work might not align with my dreams.

At least this was my experience. As a teenager, I not only wasn't sure what I wanted to do with my life, I didn't even know the kinds of questions to ask. I basically only knew that I needed a job and didn't want to do something I hated. Many young people are more thoughtful than I was. But even among the most hyper-focused people I knew, not everyone ended up doing what they had hoped. Some of my middle-aged peers still wonder what they will do when they "grow up." For others even the question of meaningful work induces anxiety. What have I done with my life? is a common question older adults ask. We all want our lives to mean something. We crave significance.

What you might fail to realize is that you don't need a "perfect" job. But you do need to be faithful and productive in ways that honor God. And simply doing that is far more beneficial than you can know. "Earned success," the fruit of any good work done well, "is a vital antidote to boredom, trauma, alienation, and depression."[1] Your work life is crucial to your flourishing. And even work conducted in what has been called the pre-prime working years, ages sixteen to twenty-four, is extremely important. During these years you will develop a "professional grammar" including "life skills, experience, resilience, rejection, success, development of a mutual cooperation instinct, the basic practice of showing up, having responsibilities and expectations."[2] These will be the building blocks upon which to build later success.

Or not.

Your working years have the potential to be either satisfying (Eccl. 2:24) or meaningless (v. 11). Some people approach all of life, including work, with a sense of mission. Others drift from task to task. Some excel at work. Others do only the bare minimum. Some properly balance work, family, and other obligations. Others are enslaved to their work or don't work enough to care for their own. How can you figure out what you are supposed to do, and then do it well?

The key to a balanced life is the Christian doctrine of calling, or its Latin equivalent *vocation*. Believers have been called by God out of the world and into his service. To "those who are called according to his purpose" (Rom. 8:28 ESV), God provides a place and time and the required gifts to fulfill his mission in the world. Or as Paul puts it: "We are his workmanship, created in Christ Jesus unto good works, which God hath before ordained that we should walk in them" (Eph. 2:10). Our unique opportunities to do God's will form our vocations, our callings. And the work you do, as a teenager or young adult, constructs the mold that will shape your later life.

In this book I aim to explain and apply vocation in three movements. First, we will *ponder* the doctrine of vocation. What does it mean to have a vocation, that is, a calling? What does Scripture teach about work? And how does the special calling of grace relate to our ordinary callings in the world? Second, we will learn how to *prepare* for vocational living. I will share what people of God at almost any stage of life can do to become better qualified to glorify and enjoy God in their various stations. What skills and character qualities will you need to be useful in the world? How can you sort through the countless vocational options? And how do you chart a course for a rewarding work life without compromising your other callings? Third, we will explore how to *practice* vocation. What biblical disciplines will help you succeed at work? How does your work life relate to the rest of who you are? And how should you steward the fruit of your labor? Finally, the last part of the book is an appendix that tackles common questions you might find yourself asking as you think about your future.

As I wrote this book, I interviewed dozens of people who exemplify godly work. Some of them are young, not much older than you might be. Others are retired and able to reflect on their careers with the advantage of hindsight. Their stories and advice are featured at the end of each chapter.

In this book you will also hear a lot of other voices. This is deliberate. Vocation is deeply embedded in the Protestant tradition. It is good to listen to how others have thought through this subject. Because I frequently include the thoughts of others, there are a lot of endnote references in the body of this text. Don't be intimidated by them. You don't have to read them. Many simply document my sources, though others suggest further reading or provide needed clarification.

Work is a weighty topic, but instead of being intimidated by it, you should treasure the rare blessing God has given to you even to consider these matters. It is easy to forget that "the majority of humans...have thrust upon them tasks and responsibilities about which they have no choice. They are in survival mode."[3] Your life sometimes feels this way. But you have far more freedom than you might realize. And if you are in a state of grace, God enables you to freely will and do eternally meaningful and rewarding things.[4]

This book is a guide for young people trying to figure out what to do with their lives. This means it is also for the parents of young people.[5] After all, as one sixteenth-century Reformed confession puts it, addressing parents, "It is necessary that [children] be taught and instructed in such studies or crafts for which they could gain an honest living, so that they would shun idleness and, above all, to be so taught that in all things they would have their true hope and trust in God alone."[6] Parents must bring their children up "in the nurture and admonition of the Lord" (Eph. 6:4). And a large part of this upbringing includes preparing for a God-honoring vocation.

I'm glad you are reading this book. This decision suggests that you are not interested in meandering through life, thoughtlessly doing the next thing thrust upon you. You want a calling, a meaningful set of responsibilities and accompanying rewards that you can call yours. Let's begin pondering this invigorating idea of calling by asking, What is vocation?

PART
ONE

PONDERING
VOCATION

WHAT IS VOCATION?

oratius Bonar was a nineteenth-century pastor. He was also a hymnist, which means he was a poet. And gifted poets have a way of using just the right words to express deep truths. In only a few lines Bonar expresses the yearning that the doctrine of vocation answers:

> Fill thou my life, O Lord my God, in ev'ry part with praise,
> That my whole being may proclaim thy being and thy ways.
> Not for the lip of praise alone, nor e'en the praising heart,
> I ask, but for a life made up of praise in ev'ry part.
>
> ...So shall no part of day or night from sacredness be free,
> But all my life, in ev'ry step, be fellowship with thee.[1]

This is what believers in Jesus want. God has called us to offer not just our minds and hearts but our bodies too as "living sacrifices" (Rom. 12:1). We want to please God not just in the few hours a week we gather with the congregation in worship but every minute of every week. Salvation frees the penitent from hell; but it also gives us ample reason to get out of bed every morning in the here and now.

It is the biblical doctrine of calling or vocation that teaches us how sacred every part of day and night is. Calling is a clear teaching of Scripture (for example, 1 Cor. 7:17–24; 2 Peter 1:3). But during the Middle Ages it was overlooked because of a radical distinction between the sacredness of church work and the commonness of all other labor. Medieval Christians thought only church workers had a vocation—everyone else simply performed jobs. The fourth-century church father Eusebius said, regrettably, that those who "have minds for farming, for trade, and the other more secular interests" have "a kind of secondary grade of piety."[2] Only church workers had first-rate godliness.[3] This false distinction was challenged by the Protestant Reformation. "Devotion," write Joel Beeke and Mark Jones, "was largely confined by medieval Catholicism to the monastery; the Reformers released it into the marketplace."[4]

We need to recover this teaching today as many modern factors threaten the reality of vocation. Secularism scorns the value of spirituality and therefore the sacredness of work. Industrialization—with its introduction of machines and the goal of making human production more machine-like—and computerization challenge the human element of our work. Globalization makes it hard to know how our earnest occupational contributions can remain untainted from more sinister motives; after all, players in a world economy have little control over how their labor is used. On top of all this, the bewildering number of occupational options can intimidate us into inaction or plague us with regret.

Because vocation is biblical, it can help us live a "life made up of praise in ev'ry part," even today.

The Basic Idea of Vocation

The French reformer John Calvin taught that calling is as simple as knowing what God wants us to do in the place that he has appointed us to live: "The Lord bids each one of us in all life's actions to look to his calling." By "calling" he means that God "has appointed duties for every man in his particular way of life." Each of us is like a guard stationed to a particular post so that we might "not heedlessly wander about throughout life." This calling from the Lord "is in everything the beginning and foundation of well-doing."[5] The father of English Puritanism William Perkins further developed the biblical theology of vocation. He defined it as "a certain kind of life, ordained and imposed on man by God for the common good."[6] The reformers agreed that "a person's 'calling' was the whole network of relationships and opportunities and duties which formed his life."[7]

In Scripture, the term *calling* almost always refers to God's call to faith, the Spirit's working of that faith, or the active life of faith. So in one sense what we call a vocation is just a part—though a large part—of our general calling to live honorably before God. Our "master-vocation" is to love the Lord supremely and our neighbor as ourselves. We do this at home, church, work, and in the public square. As a subset of our master-calling, our particular callings are how we love God and others with the skills the Lord has given us. The "main end of our lives," says Perkins, "is to serve God in serving men in the works of our callings."[8] Your vocation is the unique way in which God has chosen you to fit into his great plan.

Prior to submitting to Christ, many people lack that sense of purpose that can only be found in vital union with God (see Rom. 8:28). In other words, there is a connection between what is known as God's *effectual* call and his call to a *vocation*. Here it is: when God powerfully calls his elect by changing their hearts, he also gives them a life-calling; he enlists them in his service. After conversion, for example, tax collectors and soldiers do the same work but now with a different master and new motives (Luke 3:10–14). They are now owned by God and work for his glory. Reformation theology affirms that every Christian has a special role in this world as prophet, priest, and king.[9] Therefore, Christians have a vocation, a divine calling to serve the Lord. Calling in Scripture usually has to do with our call to faith.

But in at least one place the apostle Paul broadens the sense of Christian calling. Paul exhorts each believer to "lead the life that the Lord has assigned to him, and to which God has called him"

(1 Cor. 7:17 ESV). Paul gives the example of a bondservant who becomes a Christian through the effectual call, the gift of regeneration. Even in such a lowly station a Christian is free to serve the Lord. The German reformer Martin Luther even translated 1 Corinthians 7:20 like this: "Let every one stay in the *vocation* in which he is called."[10] Calvin understood this passage in the same way; it describes the vocations of tailors and merchants, to give just two examples.[11] According to the nineteenth-century American Presbyterian pastor Charles Hodge, Paul's wonderful point is that "the gospel is just as well suited to men in one vocation as in another."[12]

One surely does not have to become a minister to have a calling. In fact, it is essential that *not everyone* become a minister: "The Lord calls his people in *all* walks of life to follow him. He wants them to be Christian fathers and mothers, Christian husbands and wives, Christian employers and employees. Each one should fulfill the role the Lord has assigned."[13] In a sense, we are all religious workers since "we live, and move, and have our being" in God (Acts 17:28). We can do nothing that is truly areligious. So Luther could call the stations of civil government, employers, or hired workers of all sorts, "holy orders."[14] He was deliberately rejecting the Roman Catholic notion of holy orders in which only official church workers were set apart for a sacred purpose. Perkins likewise "rejected the false dichotomy between sacred and secular" and saw vocation as "the unique way" that we love God and our neighbor.[15] Puritan George Swinnock wanted the tradesman to know that "his shop as well as his chapel is holy ground."[16]

Vocation means that even bondservants, and anyone else with a hard, undesirable job, can work "heartily, as to the Lord, and not unto men." Paul reminds lowly servants that they "serve the Lord Christ" (Col. 3:22–24). There is no reason for someone doing valid work to change professions when they become a Christian—they can serve God where they are when they are called to faith: "Whatsoever ye do, do all to the glory of God" (1 Cor. 10:31). Scripture's call to every person is this: "Present your bodies as a living sacrifice, holy and acceptable to God, which is your spiritual worship" (Rom. 12:1 ESV). Calvin believed that "no sacrifice is more pleasing to God than when every man applies himself diligently to his own calling."[17]

The Christian doctrine of vocation dignifies all legitimate efforts: "All honest work is sacred when devoted to the glory of God."[18] Doing your job doesn't take you away from the work God calls you to. The workplace is where you will likely spend most of your time *in* that work he has called you to. The same is true in various degrees for labor in the family, for unpaid labor, and for engaging in civic responsibilities. After all, as Os Guinness puts it, in vocation "God calls us to himself so decisively that everything we are, everything we do, and everything we have is invested with a special devotion and dynamism lived out as a response to his summons and service."[19]

But the doctrine of vocation may not simply be assumed. It must be put into practice.

The Ingredients of a Vocation

At least three things are necessary to enjoy a vocation, a true calling from God.

A Right Perspective

The insightful twentieth-century British writer Dorothy Sayers puts it this way: The outcome of our "work will be decided by our religious outlook: as we *are* so we *make*."[20] There is a difference between how believers and unbelievers approach their varied responsibilities. Without trust in God we use opportunities to make a name for ourselves (see Gen. 11:4). Or we expect work to give us the kind of satisfaction that we can only find in Christ. We may see our jobs simply as ways to get money. But faith in God and obedience to his word can transform any valid work into worship.

Instead of inflexibly insisting on following your passions into ideal work—*I need to be an executive chef or an artist or a Navy*

Seal—as a Christian you must prioritize faith, hope, love, and patience even in roles that might be miles away from childhood dreams and current aspirations. In these situations we cheerfully live out our responsibilities before God.

Not all work is intrinsically satisfying. And all work has challenges. But a vocational outlook can help you transcend the liabilities of working in a fallen world. The Heidelberg Catechism is helpful here. Question 91 asks, "But what are good works?" Part of the answer emphasizes the perspective of the worker. Only those works are good "which are done from true faith...and for [God's] glory."[21] The various arenas of our lives—work, church, family, recreation—must be governed by trust in God and an interest in his glory. In this way, "whatever someone's station may be, faith transforms it into a vocation."[22] A vocationally minded person sees work "not, primarily, [as] a thing one does to live, but [as] the thing one lives to do."[23]

A Valid Venture

You can glorify God in whatever work you undertake, provided it is noble work. God acknowledges as vocations, according to Calvin, only "lawful modes of life, which have God as their approver and author."[24] As the Heidelberg Catechism notes, good works must be done "according to the law of God."[25] You cannot glorify God by bringing a godly attitude to an evil job. The builders of the tower of Babel worked heartily, but they lacked a valid calling because the project displeased the Lord. So, as Sayers writes, "We should ask of an enterprise, not 'will it pay?' but 'is it good?'"[26]

What tests can we apply to discover whether a job is good? Seminary professor and pastor Dan Doriani offers this answer: "Work is good...if it is moral...builds character...achieves good goals...pleases God, conforms to the structures of his world, and fits his vision of the good."[27] A job is worthy of our efforts if it harmonizes with God's original mandate that humans steward the earth in submission to him (Gen. 1:28). Legitimate work must serve God by serving people. Only if a job meets these standards can it qualify as a vocation. So some occupations cannot possibly be callings—professional gambler, loan shark (in Scripture, a usurer, or one who extorts the borrower through crippling loan terms; Ex. 22:25–27), drug dealer, pornographer, and thief, to name obvious examples.

This doesn't mean that every qualified job will *feel* like a calling. Few people washing dishes in a low-quality restaurant believe that they were born for such a job as this. But while a stepping-stone job may not be your final career, it may be the place where you will live out your faith for a time. As we will later see, you can desire vocations that meld your skills and interests to valuable and fulfilling work. But at the very least you must believe in the work you are doing. For "whatsoever is not of faith is sin" (Rom. 14:23). Still, vocational living doesn't demand work that checks all your wishlist boxes, especially early in your working life.

Faithful Work

The final ingredient of a vocation has to do with how you apply a right perspective to a valid undertaking. In other words, vocational living requires more than being a professing Christian and fulfilling legitimate opportunities. You must work well. Vocation defines not only the *why* and *where* of work, but also the *how.* Sayers sums up vocation as the calling of people "made in God's image" to "make things, as God makes them, for the sake of doing well a thing that is well worth doing."[28]

Kingdom work means not only doing quality work but also performing work in a way that honors God's command to love your neighbor as yourself (Matt. 22:39). To put it differently, you must not only produce a quality product or render excellent service. You must use your callings to love your neighbor. So Perkins wrote that a person's vocation calls him to "become a servant to his brother in all the duties of love."[29] For Christians work is not how to get ahead, clambering over the backs of others; it is how to value the interests of others (Phil. 2:4). A vocational mindset, writes pastor and author Jay Kim, "calls Christians to disrupt a culture of self-interest with sacrificial, self-giving love by leveraging skills and resources in partnership with others, for God's glory and the good of all."[30]

At work God is both the Lord of your labor and the example for your conduct. After forming and filling the world, God charged Adam to take his unique abilities and apply them earnestly and diligently to a particular plot of ground (Gen. 2:15). The plots of our lives vary but our purpose is the same: to put into practice the principles of God's kingdom in every area of life. You fulfill your vocation by living according to God's code of conduct in your various spheres of responsibility. Doriani puts it succinctly: "Truly good work uses the right means, has godly motivations, and pursues beneficial goals. Good work is both lawful and helpful to humanity."[31]

Vocation is just the doctrine you need to elevate work to its rightful place as designed by God. It is clarifying. You must work. You don't know exactly what God has planned for you, but you must be—and can be—faithful with what the Lord gives. Vocation is also invigorating. You can truly work for God no matter what you do, whether you feed cows as a farmer or feed God's people as a pastor. Because you work for God and your neighbor, you must work heartily, offering your very best. That doesn't mean that you look to your work for your value; you have that in God's love, which you receive through the gospel. So freed from sin and given a meaningful life, the doctrine of vocation is, finally, liberating. God placed us in his world to work for his glory. That is a great responsibility. But don't worry; "we as individuals aren't responsible for the world; we are just responsible for the pieces that God gives to us."[32]

Peggy ▶▶▶ Medical Lab Technician

Peggy, presently retired, worked in hospital clinical settings nearly her entire career. Her particular fields changed, but her pursuit of excellence and a devotion to serving God led her wherever she went.

Peggy explains her path this way: "I pursued a strong interest in biology after a high school project in blood typing. I was fascinated by what could be learned from blood! I majored in biology in college. Numerous laboratory projects along with excellent courses in pathogenic bacteriology and parasitology moved me to investigate medical laboratory work."

Peggy was encouraged by a college counselor to match this interest and the nature of lab work with her personality. She loved to organize, investigate, and work independently, and she had a penchant for detail—all of which complemented this type of work. She sought a post-graduate clinical year at a medical center where she could rotate through various types of laboratories. She says of that time: "I enjoyed this year immensely and after its completion, began a career!"

As a Christian, Peggy sought the Lord's guidance and doors opened right along. After four years of work experience and then viewing a magazine ad about the need for medical personnel in a new hospital being built in southern Haiti, she began what would become a ten-year term for a Christian medical group. When it was time for a native Haitian to take over her role, the Lord opened a door for her to return to the States for further education, this time in general biblical studies. She closed out her working years serving with an organization that provided lab equipment to underfunded clinics around the world. The team delivered and installed equipment, trained technicians in instrument use, and instructed them in good laboratory practice.

At every stage of her career, Peggy knew the Lord's leading. Though the Lord never gave her a spouse and a family of her own, she could still say, "God gave deep satisfaction and blessing. There were difficult days and discouragements, particularly in Haiti, but always his faithful presence."

WHAT IS WORK?

God calls his chosen people to rest in him and then to work for him. You can't work to earn God's favor; salvation is "not of works, lest any man should boast" (Eph. 2:9). But you can show your gratitude by doing the good works that God has prepared for you to walk in (v. 10). Christians are workers. And the good works that you must do are not only "special" works of charity, like going on a service trip or volunteering at a shelter. All of life offers opportunities to perform good work that flows from faith, conforms to God's law, and tends to God's glory.[1] So clearly your work life is an arena for good works. Work is not only a valid expression of vocation but a large part of it. After all, "work gets the largest single block of our lives."[2]

We could define work simply as labor or toil. But British pastor John Stott offers a more expansive definition. Work is "the expenditure of manual or mental energy in service, which brings fulfillment to the worker, benefit to the community, and glory to God."[3] This is helpful. Work is toil. But it is toil to a purpose. And it is done in relation to the God who made us.

To gain a right perspective of the work to which you are called, you should understand its story and purpose.

The Story of Work

The Bible is a story of work. Scripture's first verb is a synonym for work. "In the beginning God created" (Gen. 1:1). God produced. He made. The Bible also ends with God at work. Jesus says, "Surely, I come quickly" (Rev. 22:20). Jesus will finish his work of redemption soon. When Jesus' enemies persecuted him for healing even on the Sabbath, he gave this defense: "My Father is working until now, and I am working" (John 5:17 ESV). God is a worker. This truth from the story of work reveals the first lesson about work.

Work Is Good

Obviously, God's work is good. As the Belgic Confession puts it, God is "good, and the overflowing fountain of all good."[4] God himself affirmed his work of creation; "it was very good" (Gen. 1:31). Because of its goodness the Lord can "rejoice in his works" (Ps. 104:31). God's good work is the foundation for our belief in the goodness of all valid industry.

Human work, too, can be good. We know this because early in the story of God's work he made people to work with him (Gen. 2:15; 1 Cor. 3:9). By making us in his image God gave us a calling to work. God formed and filled the earth with good things. And he created people to cultivate it, to "work the ground" (Gen. 2:5 ESV). We were made to subdue the earth and have "dominion over... every living thing" in it (Gen. 1:28). "Through work we respond to our unique human calling to extend by human creativity the work of God begun in Creation."[5]

Throughout the Bible God celebrates and memorializes all sorts of human work. Just four chapters into God's revelation he notes diverse kinds of production that he providentially uses for his good purposes: crop farming (Gen. 2:15; 4:3), animal care (2:19; 4:2, 20), city building (4:17), the making and playing of musical instruments (v. 21), the forging of bronze and iron tools (v. 22), and homemaking (vv. 25–26). God commands work and provides a reward for good labor (Ex. 20:9; Ps. 128:2; Prov. 31:31). Work is more than a way to get by in a broken world; it is a positive good.

But it wasn't long after God created man and put him to work that the story of work took a dark turn.

Work Is Tarnished by Sin

The degradation of work is inevitable. Sin and the fall hurt everything, but especially human work. The woman's work of childbearing and homemaking would become painful and contentious (Gen. 3:16). The man's work to feed his family and manage the earth would be toilsome. God told the first man, "Cursed is the ground because of you; in pain you shall eat of it all the days of your life...By the sweat of your face you shall eat bread" (3:17, 19 ESV).

Both workers and the goods they produce and services they render are plagued by the effects of sin. In your work you might get slivers and smashed fingernails, underbid projects, or have your plans rejected by superiors or clients. The homes you build might get leaky roofs and become infested by termites. You will forget important meetings. Coworkers will gossip about you. You will bring wrong expectations to your job and sometimes work poorly. If your work is judged unacceptable or unnecessary, you might get fired.

Vocation does not rescue labor from its hardships. Solomon calls the work that we are to be busy with a "sore travail" (Eccl. 1:13), "an unhappy business" (ESV), a "burdensome task" (NKJV). You need a realistic view of work. Your dream job will never be all that you want it to be; expecting it to be so is one of the most dangerous things about post-fall work. Like other good but imperfect things, work can become an idol. It promises honor, comfort, stability, and wealth. But work and its fruits will always disappoint.

Because of the fall, some work is so twisted from God's original design that Christians cannot do it. Not all work is legitimate. Making metal pipes can be good work. Making metal idols is sin (Acts 19:24–25). Being a loan officer can fulfill the need for housing. Being a payday loan shark only further burdens the poor (see Neh. 5:10).

Work is good, but broken. Still, God is merciful.

Work Is Restored by God's Mercy

Adam and Eve failed miserably in their stewardship over creation. Instead of ruling over the serpent they became his servants, and so God cursed the ground that Adam was called to work. But God did not retract Adam and Eve's vocation. Instead, he promised to send them a savior who would fully do God's will, and he charged them to combat the curse with all their strength.

This is your calling too. In fact, it is the reality of sin's effects that makes Christian vocational excellence so necessary. Believers bring gospel hope into broken systems of work. We resist abuse, injustice, and oppression. We reject fears that God is unable to provide for his people. We renounce shoddy work, certain that God is worthy of our best. We work motivated not by greed but by gratitude. Our work is a way of promoting God's goodness even in a fallen world. And though toil can be disappointing, God kindly rewards our labors.

Think about it in the big picture of the story of Scripture. Because of our sin, work is not what it once was before the fall. But because of God's kindness it *is* valuable. God honors even hard or unpleasant labor as a means of caring for us, our families, and those who benefit from our production and generosity. Your work can reflect the good work of God. You can find fulfillment in your production and find joy in it. You can even use the degree of futility built into all human activity to rest in God's perfect work: since you cannot toil your way into paradise, you must wait for God to restore all things, even the beauty of your labor. In the age to come human labor will be released from vanity and bondage (Rom. 8:9–21). But our calling to work will not be nullified.[6] As pastor Tom Nelson puts it, "Your time here in our Father's fallen world is a preparation for an eternity of activity and creativity."[7]

Work isn't a curse but a calling, our echo to God's goodness. And this is true for all Christian workers. Martin Luther was vehement: "The works of monks and priests, however holy and arduous they may be, do not differ one whit in the sight of God from the works of the rustic laborer in the field or the woman going about her household tasks...all works are measured before God by faith alone."[8] The doctrine of vocation doesn't make labor easy. But it does infuse our work "with a religious and social value that dignifies it."[9]

Now that we know the story of work, we can better understand why we do it.

The Reasons for Work

Needing to work is not, of course, a uniquely Christian concern. The demands of life require even the most ungodly and carefree to produce at least enough to stay alive. But as a Christian you have higher reasons to get to work and to do it well.

Work to Honor God

Work is a divine law. God requires human labor. On multiple occasions Paul instructed the Thessalonian believers: "Do your own business, and...work with your own hands" (1 Thess. 4:11). If a person refuses to work, the church should not subsidize his disobedience (2 Thess. 3:10). Image-bearers must work because God works. Even if you had no financial need, God would still require you to be diligent. And God gives you a place to apply your talents.

Of course God doesn't need your work. You are easily replaceable on the job; this truth should keep you humble. Still, until God replaces you, you are to cultivate the ground that God values. Vocational disobedience is sin. Refusing to use your gifts in a noble calling "is not only contrary to nature but also to the will of God."[10]

A sometimes-forgotten consequence of work is that it can help keep us out of trouble. The apostle Paul had heard rumors that some in the Thessalonian church walked "disorderly, working not at all, [and were] busybodies" (2 Thess. 3:11). His remedy? Such persons "we command and exhort by our Lord Jesus Christ, that with quietness they work, and eat their own bread" (v. 12). This command is urgent because, as Leland Ryken writes, "Work...is not just a task that is completed; it is part of a believer's relationship to God."[11]

Work to Meet Your Own Needs

God made people to flourish; poverty is a consequence of sin and a sign that not all is well. So it is right that we work for our own good (Prov. 10:4). This is another reason why Paul disallows the Christian community to feed the lazy; by refusing to provide for his own needs, the lazy man threatens the flourishing of the community. Lester De Koster puts it plainly: "The Bible views refusal to work as theft" (see Eph. 4:28).[12] Sloth is sin for which God has no patience. Laziness is more than mere insufficient productivity; "it is a condition of explicitly spiritual dejection that has given up on the pursuit of God, the true, the good, and the beautiful."[13] In Jesus' parable of the talents, the servant who buried his one talent in the earth was wicked because he was slothful (Matt. 25:26). Vocation is practical; we need livelihoods to survive. And we mustn't needlessly burden our neighbors by inadequate production.

Work to Serve Others

Under God's blessing diligent labor leads to abundance (Prov. 21:5). Honest work often provides a surplus that one may "share with anyone in need," beginning with those closest to him but including others as opportunity allows (Eph. 4:28 ESV; Gal. 6:10). Faithful work for honest pay is an obvious way that our work serves others—compensation proves that our neighbor values our labor.

But even the work itself, aside from its pay, is rewarding. Lester De Koster writes, "Work gives meaning to life because work is the way in which we make ourselves useful to society."[14] We "make ourselves useful" by using our gifts—gifts that were given to us by the Spirit "for the common good" (1 Cor. 12:7 ESV). If you work well, you are doing more good for others than you might realize. I found a children's book in our church library called *How God Gives Us Bread*. It opens with a boy and a girl eating sandwiches around a table. On the wall hangs a framed picture of the fourth petition of the Lord's prayer, "Give us this day our daily bread" (Matt. 6:11). The children ask their mother how God does this. Mom takes the children on a field trip to see farmers plowing, planting, and harvesting; millers grinding; bakers baking; drivers delivering; and store clerks selling. Each of these workers were serving the children, and others, by putting bread on their table.[15] A similar story could be written about your work. This is what William Perkins has in mind when he writes, "God manifests His fatherly care over us by the employment of men in His service according to their several vocations for our good" (see Ps. 127:1; 1 Cor. 3:6).[16] To put it negatively, your physical and mental gifts remain fruitless unless you use them to serve others in your calling.

You are "labourers together with God" (1 Cor. 3:9). God cares for his world through his generous providence (Matt. 5:45); your good work is an instrument of divine providence through which God demonstrates his goodness and through which you love your neighbor through tangible service (v. 44). You should come to work not to be served but to serve, believing that it is truly "more blessed to give than to receive" (Acts 20:35; see Mark 12:43–45).

Work to Witness

Work is both where and how we show others the practical power of the gospel in everyday life. Serious Christians want to tell others the "reason of the hope that is in" them (1 Pet. 3:15; Job 32:19–20). But, as Dutch missionary "Brother" Andrew van der Bijl put it, "There's an art to witnessing by your presence." And too many professing believers lack that art. "The problem with Western Christians is not that they aren't *where* they should be but that they aren't *what* they should be where they are."[17] The way you work must open rather than close doors to speak about Jesus, and it must give those to whom you witness opportunity to glorify rather than despise God.

It is wrong to evangelize *in place of* working; stealing your employer's time under the banner of religion does not "adorn the doctrine of God our Saviour" (Titus 2:10). But God can use our faithful living—including our vocational faithfulness—to win our neighbors over for Christ (Matt. 5:16). People who work like God are literally remarkable, worthy of remark. As Jay Kim writes, "To an unbelieving world languishing in the toil of transactional work, it should spark curiosity toward the possibility of something more, something holy."[18] What explanation is there, for example, when you return good for your coworker's evil or lend without any expectation of return (Matt. 5:39–42)?

Work to Become Conformed to Christ

Work is a large part of how and where you take up your cross to follow Jesus. "The setting for spiritual battle," says Michael Berg, "is vocation."[19]

Your work forces you to trust God. You labor. But you must also pray that God will establish the work of your hands (Ps. 90:17) and redeem your labor from vanity (127:1).[20] At work you must stand up for justice even if you stand alone. You must practice submission (1 Pet. 2:12–17). On the job you might "endure grief, suffering wrongly" (v. 19). You work for superiors who are often unappreciative. You bring home a paycheck to people who may not thank you. Yet God's children endure (v. 20).

Will you take up your cross and follow Christ in your vocation? I will later suggest that we must prepare for our working lives by developing Christlike characters. But work itself forms who we are becoming: "God has so made us that through working we actually sculpt the kind of selves we each are becoming, in time and for eternity."[21] Because we spend so much time working, our choices on the job mold us more than we realize. Do you show up on time every day? Do you cheerfully accept the work others refuse? Do you resist accepting on-the-job "perks" (like eating the food you are assembling in the back of the restaurant)? These decisions to work well, though seemingly small, are shaping your character. This reality prompted De Koster to write that "self is in fact by far the most important product we produce in the life and time granted us by divine grace."²²

We should follow Christ's example in the fulfillment of our vocations (1 Pet. 2:21). But no matter how hard you try, you will fail at work. Yet even your vocational failures can conform you to Christ if they drive you to trust that "he himself bore our sins in his body on the tree, that we might die to sin and live to righteousness. By his wounds you have been healed" (v. 24 ESV). One acquaintance, who works in the service industry in an environment radically hostile to Christianity, offered this reflection: "I can either dwell on all the aspects of this job that I don't like—trust me, there are many—or I can choose to surrender each day to the Lord and pray that he helps me find joy in the purpose that he has given me here."

Work is hard. But it is good. Mere human labor is vain; laboring in the Lord never is (1 Cor. 15:58). As we work, much seems crooked, unable to be straightened (Eccl. 1:15). The students you teach don't seem to listen. The lawns you mow grow right back, sometimes with unsightly weeds. But Scripture counsels you to work with all your heart (9:10), leaving the results to God. Theologian Earnst Hengstenberg offers rich advice: "The best thing of all, is to build and confide heartily on God, to commit the ordering of all to Him, to let Him rule, to pray as the Lord taught us—'thy kingdom come.'" In this fallen world,

> do the work with which thou art entrusted, apply thyself with all industry to thy calling: all else that refuses to be rectified, leave to Him who is stronger and wiser than thou, to the good God in Heaven who can rule churches, country, people, princes, house, estate, wife and children better than thou.²³

You must work. But remember, God is working, even through you, "to do...his good pleasure" (Phil. 2:13).

Mike ▶▶▶ Daycare Owner

Mike is an entrepreneur. He started, owns, and directs First Things Childcare, a private Christian daycare in Montana. Mike believes strongly in the necessity of direct parental involvement, but in a fallen world, his service is valuable. So, he daily takes on the delegated responsibility for the care, safety, and training of a dozen little kids. He puts in long hours—7:00 a.m. to 6:00 p.m. Monday through Friday—and has no outside financial backers. It is a lot of work, but according to Mike, it is exhilarating!

Mike modeled his business after a husband/wife team who started and operated five daycares. He read manuals on this kind of a startup. But it took fourteen years from the time he considered the idea to when his business opened. During that time he "experienced a lot of professional failure," which turned out, in hindsight, to be an excellent teaching tool. Mike worked at a daycare for sixteen months, where he identified ways that his own center could excel. For example, many daycares rely on movies and tablets to "pacify and babysit the kids throughout the day." Mike says, "My daycare is completely screen free. That has a tremendously positive effect on the kids, and the parents love it." First Things Childcare is explicitly Christian. Mike teaches Bible lessons and sings Christian songs with the kids.

Like all Christian workers, Mike must fulfill his vocation as a representative of Christ. In his work this means being patient with small children (as they misbehave or tell a too-long story about a visit with Grandpa). He must be diligent to respond to emails from interested parents and be attentive to the facility. He knows he will fall short. But, he says, "The gospel sets me free from 'what if' panic. Christ's mercies are new every morning. He forgives our sins and changes us daily to be more like him."

HOW IS CALLING RELATED TO CONVERSION?

Every believer has a vocation, a calling to glorify God in his or her station. In the Lord's sovereign distribution, according to our unique callings, we must walk (1 Cor. 7:17). Our specific callings—mechanic, pilot, housewife—flow from the general calling to be a Christian and from the effectual call of the Holy Spirit. And thus there is an essential relationship between calling and conversion.

This is not to discredit the significant work done by non-believers. John Calvin puts it this way: "Hardly anyone is to be found who does not manifest talent in some art," either liberal or manual. God bestows his gifts "indiscriminately upon pious and impious... the mind of man, though fallen and perverted from its wholeness, is nevertheless clothed and ornamented with God's excellent gifts." Even the "natural person" (1 Cor. 2:14 ESV) can be "sharp and penetrating in their investigation" of natural things.[1] God helps his children, says Calvin, through the "work and ministry of the ungodly" in physics, logical argumentation, mathematics, and many other fields.[2] In the diversity of gifts, Calvin writes, God grants even to unbelievers "some remaining traces of the image of God, which distinguish the entire human race from the other creatures."[3] Non-Christians can work well. And I'm thankful for this. When I step onto an airplane, I don't first wonder if the pilot knows his catechism, but if he is a master of his craft!

Despite all this, unbelievers do not self-consciously live out a calling. They can't. In all areas of life, including work, they do not honor the Lord as God (Rom. 1:21). William Perkins gets to the point: "The *person* must first please God before the *work* of the person please him. 'For to the unclean, all things are unclean' (Titus 1:15)."[4] An unconverted person simply cannot live vocationally, bringing the truth of God to bear on every area of life. If you want to live out a Christian calling, you have to actually be a Christian. Or, as Perkins puts it, "Every man must join the practice of his personal calling with the practice of the general calling of Christianity."[5]

It will be helpful if you consider some of the many ways that a true conversion to Christ enables you to live out your vocations, be it in a paid occupation, or as a parent, a student, or a volunteer. You "must be born again" to both "see the kingdom of God" (John 3:7, 3) and to live as a good citizen of that kingdom.

Conversion Answers Our Need for Justification

Not everyone will admit it, but work can become a useless quest for purpose and value. Tom Nelson writes, "Hard work, however noble, without a relationship with the Father proves empty, meaningless, and despairing."[6] We are tempted to think that we will matter when our work is helpful, appreciated, and financially well compensated. Even professing Christians can forget to apply the gospel of free grace to their vocational life. We can say that "by the grace of God I am what I am" (1 Cor. 15:10), but we might still feel that God truly loves us only when we meet high standards of performance at church, home, and work. We have a felt need for work to justify our lives. We want our work to mean something.

The converting grace of God frees us from the treadmill of justification-seeking performance. Here's how one writer on vocation describes the way divine justification through faith in Christ freed him to live like a son rather than a slave: "With heaven secure and my livelihood in good hands (God's hands), I looked up and saw my neighbor. I was set free to lose myself in the craft of my vocation. I was free to love both my job and my people."[7] Andrew, a friend in the insurance business, puts it this way: "Because of the gospel and knowing that I am justified, I am free to love and serve my neighbor." God "frees Christians from working for him"—like a servant seeking affirmation—"so that they can work for their neighbors."[8]

Grace assures us that we don't have to become anything for God to accept us. If he has given us his Son, then he will "freely give us all things" (Rom. 8:32). The first truth about you as a believer is not that you are a worker, or a provider, or an achiever, but that Christ loves you and has given himself for you (Gal. 2:20)! This is vital. As devotional writer Oswald Chambers puts it, "The greatest competitor of true devotion to Jesus is the service we do for Him." Before you can truly work for God you must be satisfied in him.[9]

If you are not bringing God's love into your work, your vocational life will make little impact. It will be selfish and unsatisfying. You will be ruled by fear of man and a greedy desire for more. Only God's free grace unlocks your true potential to glorify and enjoy God in your work.

Conversion Activates the Motivator of Gratitude

Teacher and scholar Douglas Schuurman writes that "ingratitude is a chief obstacle to experiencing life as vocation. Ingratitude is the blind refusal to acknowledge with thanks the gifted character of life and of God."[10] Without gratitude for the gift of new life, we are not ready and willing to live for God.

Only when God redeems us can we finally receive all his gifts, including our callings—even their challenging aspects—as gifts deserving of profound thankfulness. Schuurman goes on to say that "the stunning clarity of the gift of God's own Son jars our eyes open, enabling us to see the rest of reality anew, so that its extraordinarily gifted character is finally recognized."[11] Only when Paul met Christ did he say, "What shall I do, Lord?" (Acts 22:10). The Christian no longer belongs to himself: "You are not your own, for you were bought with a price. So glorify God in your body" (1 Cor. 6:19–20 ESV).

The best work—the only truly God-glorifying work—is performed out of gratitude to God. And this is true no matter how difficult or seemingly fruitless the task. Puritan John Flavel is right: "To have an honest and lawful employment, in which you do not dishonour God in benefiting [yourself], is no small mercy."[12] Our work is not how we say please—God, give me the reward of my labor. Instead it is how we say thank you.

The last five chapters of the book of Romans build on Paul's earlier doctrinal instruction by giving much practical application for our lives and vocations. This section begins with this powerful phrase: "I appeal to you therefore, brothers, by the mercies of God, to present your bodies as a living sacrifice, holy and acceptable to God, which is your spiritual worship" (Rom. 12:1 ESV). The Heidelberg Catechism beautifully captures this truth: because I "belong to my faithful Saviour Jesus Christ...by His Holy Spirit, he also assures me of eternal life, and makes me heartily willing and ready henceforth to live unto him."[13] To live and die in the joy of divine comfort I need to know "how I am to be thankful to God for such redemption."[14] We do good works, not to be justified by God but, as Luther wrote, "out of spontaneous love in obedience to God."[15] The gospel tells us that all of life is a gift and an opportunity to thank God for that gift. That truth can change your work life.

Conversion Imparts Essential Vocational Qualities and Convictions

Working well—by faith, according to law, for God's glory—requires a radical change in how we think.

Good work requires the fruit of the Spirit. We must "grow in grace, and in the knowledge of our Lord and Saviour Jesus Christ"

(2 Pet. 3:18) and be "transformed by the renewing of [our] minds" (Rom. 12:2). We can do that only after God converts us. God begins and continues our work of transformation by the Spirit who indwells his people and bears life-changing fruit (Gal. 5:22–23). And we can take this fruit to work.

For example, you need love; it isn't enough to love your work, you also need to love the people with and for whom you work.

You need joy—not mere satisfaction when a project works out or when your coworkers help you to have a good time, but deep happiness in God that transcends whatever is happening on the job.

You need peace; justification by faith gives you peace with God even when there is war at work (Rom. 5:1). Only justified people can say, "God is our refuge and strength, a very present help in trouble" (Ps. 46:1).

You need patience; if God is calmly working out his plan in your life, you do not need to rush ahead of his providence. Similar things could be said for kindness, goodness, faithfulness, gentleness, and self-control. Only "they that are Christ's" can crucify sinful passions and desires and "put on the new man" who alone is able to face the spiritual challenges of vocation (Gal. 5:24; Eph. 4:24).

Good work also requires convictions informed by sound theology. Homespun vocational platitudes and clichés—if you can dream it, you can do it; there's a "U" in success—won't do. Only convictional fortitude founded on God's word can revolutionize your work life. To work well you need to take your theology to work! Conversion gives you "the mind of Christ" (1 Cor. 2:16), which enables you to think and act like God in even the hardest times.

Conversion Enables Us to Truly Love Our Neighbor

Vocation is a call to love your neighbor in fulfillment of God's law (Gal. 5:14; Rom. 13:10). As Douglas Schuurman writes, this means that we should interpret God's general call to love others in relation to particular obligations God calls us to fulfill in our friendships, paid work, marriages, and families. In all of them God's general call is applied and made specific, showing where and how God wants each of us to love our neighbor.[16]

Christians live for others, renouncing selfish ambition and honoring the significance of our neighbors (Phil. 2:3). Luther gets at this truth on the topic of good works in his Small Catechism: "A good work is everything that a child of God does, speaks, or thinks in faith according to the Ten Commandments, for the glory of God, for the benefit of his neighbor."[17]

Before conversion, however, we are hateful, not loving (Titus 3:3–4). Even Christians must admit, in the words of the Heidelberg Catechism, "I am by nature prone to hate God and my neighbor."[18] You can't work well if you are bent on hatred.

When God pours his love into our hearts, it overflows into the lives of others, even at work (Rom. 5:5). We love others because God loves us (see 1 John 4:19–21). Here's how this works in vocation according to Michael Berg: Free from striving to satisfy God, "my energy is geared toward this life. And if my energy is used in a variety of vocations...then I am always neighbor-oriented," focused on others.[19] I look to their interests before mine (Phil. 2:4). I happily take unwanted shifts. I gladly mentor less-experienced colleagues. I view my colleagues as more than workers and take an interest in their personal needs. J.C. Ryle enlarges Jesus' words in Matthew 20:28. "True greatness consists, not in receiving, but in giving,—not in selfish absorption of good things, but in imparting good to others,—not in being served, but in serving,—not in sitting still and being ministered to, but in going about and ministering to others."[20] You will only love like this if you become changed by trusting in Christ and resting in his goodness.

Conversion Empowers Vocational Witnessing

Work is one of the more obvious places believers testify to their hope in God (1 Pet. 3:15). The fall inflicts on work harsh realities that can create a sense of workplace drudgery: "It is an unhappy business that God has given to the children of men to be busy with" (Eccl. 1:13 ESV).

Christians witness at work through hope in God. And hope is more than a positive attitude or a strong work ethic. Hope is living in the expectation of future good. In Christian terms, hope is confidence in the full experience of salvation. This hope is already becoming reality. Because hope is grounded in the ongoing work of Christ, it "offers a coherent and energizing basis for [our] work in today's world." Resurrection life changes everything: "Jesus is raised, so God's new creation has begun—and we, his followers, have a job to do!"[21]

Your calling at work and elsewhere is to preview to your neighbors the beauty of the kingdom. You can't accept the status quo if it is at odds with kingdom principles. That means you must fully show up for work because God is worthy of your best. You must stand up for a bullied coworker even if he is unpopular, because to do so is Godlike. You should accept tasks that others find demeaning—so did Jesus (John 13:14). All of this countercultural vocational activity stands out because it shows how God is at work.

Work can be like the black canvas of a night sky on which the actions of believers can "shine as lights in the world" (Phil. 2:15). To use Paul's example, even at work believers refuse to grumble or dispute (v. 14), distinguishing them from their coworkers. What can explain such otherworldly activity? Christians believe that the God who creates and redeems also continues to work in this world. The King is on the throne, so we have no reason to complain or argue. To witness at work through words and actions, you need a real, personal experience of grace.

Conversion Promises Vocational Growth

God's justification of sinners—his gracious declaration that believers are righteous in Christ—is always linked to his sanctification of those same believers. By sanctification God renews in the image of Christ justified and regenerated sinners and enables them to walk in the good works God prepared for them. This means, as theologian Herman Hoeksema puts it, that believers are both "sanctified in principle and liberated from the dominion of sin" and are "continually sanctified by the Spirit of God."[22] God dethrones sin in the hearts of justified believers—once for all. Sin no longer controls us. We no longer take comfort in it. We still struggle against sin, but sin will not have the victory.

You must diligently pursue Christlikeness, but it is God who sanctifies (1 Thess. 5:23). God works in believers "both to will and to do of his good pleasure" (Phil. 2:13). "*Because* God works we work," writes John Murray.[23]

Because sin has made work hard and often unpleasant, sanctification is a massive vocational encouragement for believers. By his divine power God will give you everything you need to work in godliness (2 Pet. 1:3). Sometimes your schedule will seem impossible. The work is grueling or boring. Your job hurts your body or your pride. You feel like complaining or arguing. The temptations for pride or sloth are great. And believers are grieved by their own sin at work. We know we are forgiven but hate what we keep on doing (Rom. 7:15). If you are in Christ, God isn't finished working on you. Christ will perfect what he has begun (Phil. 1:6). You won't be "made perfect in holiness" until death.[24] But in Christ God is moving you toward perfection in holiness even now, even at work.

Conversion Guarantees Vocational Reward

Your work is valuable. This is true whether you are turning a wrench, trading stocks, or fulfilling classroom obligations. Even secular people would say that. But in the Christian worldview work is valuable not simply because of its sincerity or societal contribution, but because it actually pleases God. Yes, your work is a little like the scrawled artwork or the dandelion bouquet of a little child—the Father loves it not because it is perfect but because it came from his dear child. And all the good works that God's children do are done in Christ. Every believer can say with Paul, "The life which I now live in the flesh I live by the faith of the Son of God" (Gal. 2:20). Believers are united to Christ in his death and resurrection (Rom. 6:5). We "walk in newness of life" in him (v. 4). Our works are good—our *work* is good—because Christ is working in us. His righteousness so overrules our flaws that God is pleased by the good that we do. It is a powerful reality: We not only *must* glorify God; our work actually *does* glorify him (Rom. 8:8–9)!

On the last day each redeemed person will be like the little child who presents to a parent a smudged drawing—we know it isn't very good work even though we've done it sincerely—and God will say, "Well done" (Luke 19:17 ESV)! On that day, as the Belgic Confession teaches, the "righteous and the elect" will "receive the fruits of their labor" and the faithful "shall be crowned with glory and honor."[25] Because of God's grace your work will actually be extolled on the last day. Not because you did it without defect but because you did it in Christ!

You can trust that God is working through you: "Even if you do not seem to 'make a difference,' he makes a difference. And you may not be able to see it. So...take him at his Word."[26]

All of God's creatures must work. Even animals labor for the Lord (see Ex. 8; Num. 22:28; 1 Kings 17:3–4). But sin has especially marred human work. Naturally born people work for wrong reasons and in wrong ways. Sin disorients every part of us. Everything we put our hands and minds to is tainted by sin. But Christ has come to reverse the curse. Satan's rebellion is doomed to fail. Earth will be remade. And, gloriously, Christ is redeeming the elect and their work. Conversion equips the called to fulfill their calling.

Philosopher and Reformed theologian Paul Helm reminds us that when a person is called by grace, although he has a new nature, and is for that reason no longer 'of the world' (I Cor. 2:12) yet he is still in the world...Although he is destined for another world, the believer's first responsibility lies in this world.

A person effectually called by God sees his life "as a calling to be fulfilled for the glory of God, a theatre in which he is to engage in Christian warfare and in which the renewal of God's image in him takes place."[27] We are called to someone—God—before we are called to something—the various tasks that he has for us. "Secondary callings matter, but only because the primary calling matters most," writes Os Guinness.[28] As a Christian you can work for God in the world because he is working in and through you.

Abigail ►►► Executive Assistant and Financial Operations Associate

Abigail serves in the office of a wealth management company in New York City. She wasn't looking for this kind of work, but after graduating in the midst of the COVID pandemic in 2020, through referrals she was able to find the job that she absolutely loves.

If she wasn't preparing for this kind of work, how did she become equipped for the endurance and high standard of excellence her job requires? "Working in customer service definitely helped," she says, "but my college career in humanities and involvement in my church prepared me most."

In a current work climate characterized by transience Abigail has helpful advice: "Flourishing in a job is not always found by working in your supposed 'passion.' It can be harder but often more rewarding to stay in one place and work through the challenges of a job. Don't be tempted to make rash decisions. Take time to think about advice on a career shift if it's completely necessary." She encourages workers not to be afraid to ask for help if they feel they aren't flourishing at their job.

When it comes to witnessing as a worker, Abigail offers the following testimony: "When we're on the job, I keep my head down and work, as a means of exemplifying a good work ethic and not detracting from my colleagues' tasks. When we're socializing or at work events, those are the times where I often get to open up about my faith."

PART
TWO

PREPARING
FOR YOUR
VOCATION

HAVE SOMETHING
TO OFFER

Work is an exchange. We give labor in return for an appropriate reward. The compensation isn't always a paycheck. Fathers and mothers give themselves in the hope of being rewarded with honorable children (Prov. 15:20; 29:15). A similar principle holds true for volunteer work. Not all work pays the bills, but all worthy labor is undertaken with the aim of bearing fruit for yourself or others.

Of course, this is not how we work for God. We approach him not as workers demanding compensation (Rom. 4:1–5), but as servants of the Most High (Luke 17:10) and children held in his firm fatherly hand (Matt. 6:26). But the fact that Paul, in Romans 4, must differentiate how we approach God confirms the transactional nature of ordinary labor. When we work for others, we expect a good return for our diligence.

Here's the problem: many people feel entitled to a good life no matter what they give in exchange. They might assume, often illogically, that they will have a better standard of living than their parents. But many people think too little of what they have to offer the world, what they bring to the bargaining table. Put bluntly, "You need to be good at something before you can expect a good job."[1]

And this is not an unspiritual matter. Being "good at something" is lauded in the Scriptures from cover to cover. Proverbs 31 is a prime example. It is no wonder that the virtuous woman's household flourished; she is a picture of godly wisdom, character, and competence. What we should ask is, How did she *become* the premier example of everything taught in the previous thirty chapters of Proverbs? How can young people come to have something to offer?

I'm not talking about setting your sights on a stellar career from a young age and ruthlessly attacking impressive goals until you achieve your dream. Few young people can self-consciously prepare for the precise careers that will occupy most of their lives. And you don't have to put that kind of pressure on yourself. Many successful people didn't know what they would do with their lives until they were well beyond their younger years. I sure didn't. Norm, the president of a Canadian robotics company, told me, "I always tell younger people to not try to script their career moves too specifically. Instead, be available to take on something that is important to the business, even if it is not your ideal move." That is good advice.

Still, youth is a time of vocational preparation. In fact, preparing for the future is basic to the present vocation of young people—this was even true for the Son of God, as we'll see. There are at least three basic goals young people must pursue to have something to offer the world in their future vocations. They correspond to what you know, who you are, and what you can do. And they have glimmers of commonality with Jesus' increase "in wisdom and stature, and in favour with God and man" (Luke 2:52).

Gain Wisdom (What You Know)

The pursuit of wisdom is fundamental to the biblical disciple. Solomon told his son what he had heard from his father: the most important thing you can do is "get wisdom, get understanding;" and, once you have gotten wisdom, you should "exalt her" (Prov. 4:5, 8).

Even the boy Jesus "increased in wisdom" (Luke 2:52). Astonishingly, Jesus the *man* practiced more wisdom than Jesus the *child*. His early childishness wasn't sinful, but it was capable of maturity. And it is significant that Luke's note on Jesus' maturity in wisdom is a bridge from his youth to the start of his public vocation as mediator. Something similar is said of Samuel: "And the child Samuel grew on, and was in favour both with the Lord, and also with men" (1 Sam. 2:26). In the next chapter he is called into service; he begins his vocation.

It is not an exaggeration to say that wisdom is the most important thing you bring to God's work. You can develop into a better worker, but only if you are wise. So Solomon says to the young: "Wisdom is the principal thing; therefore get wisdom. And in all your getting, get understanding" (Prov. 4:7 NKJV).

Wisdom is not the same as knowledge. Reformed theologian Herman Bavinck makes an important distinction: "Genuine wisdom is not the product of human intellect but [is] rooted in the fear of the Lord and consists in the moral discipline that conforms to the law of the Lord and manifests itself in a moral life."[2] But wisdom and knowledge are closely related. By wisdom we use the knowledge we have gained to pursue the best ends by the best means. By wisdom we rightly evaluate who we are and the gifts God has given us and the responsibilities he has laid upon us; only then can we live well before his face. We are better equipped to practice wisdom through the accumulation of true knowledge that is as deep and broad as possible. So, the pursuit of wisdom requires you to store up knowledge to use later under the oversight of a heart ruled by God.

This means that your vocational training has everything to do with your life as a student. The young person who says or otherwise demonstrates that he doesn't care about his education demeans the doctrine of calling. Many of the adults I surveyed in writing this book lamented not working harder in school. And for good reason. Part of what made Moses "mighty in words and in deeds" was his prior rigorous academic training (Acts 7:22).

Likewise, as a young man Daniel was "in all matters of wisdom and understanding…ten times better" than his peers (Dan. 1:20). It was his wisdom that made him useful to the king of Babylon. It was Paul's serious work as a student under Gamaliel that allowed him later to confound the religious scholars of his day (Gal. 1:14). The disciple Apollos was, doubtless, catechized in the truths of general revelation in Alexandria, Egypt and "in the way of the Lord" (Acts 18:24, 25). Thus prepared, he "greatly helped" the church (v. 27 ESV).

You don't have to be a top-tier scholar. But you must "grow in the grace and knowledge of our Lord and Savior" (2 Pet. 3:18 ESV). Critiquing evangelical anti-intellectualism, historian Mark Noll pleads that you must learn to "think like a Christian," making "an effort to take seriously the sovereignty of God over the world he created, the lordship of Christ over the world he died to redeem, and the power of the Holy Spirit over the world he sustains each and every moment."[3] Sadly, many young people don't. As a result, too few are prepared for the thought-war raging in our world. Os Guinness is right: in general, evangelicals are "worldlier and more culturally shortsighted than we realize."[4] And due to a careless response to the digital revolution, many Christians are in danger of having minds "wrecked by constant distraction and unfamiliar with concentration."[5] That is unwise.

In your occupations you will be tested to your breaking point. The best way to enter the workforce is by developing a worldview that is up to the challenges the world will throw at you. Don't be tricked by the Pharisees' claim that Peter and John were "unlearned and ignorant men." True, the disciples lacked snooty academic credentials. But they were educated; for three years "they had been with Jesus" (Acts 4:13). We too must train our hearts and minds in communion with Christ, believing that it is "much better to get wisdom than gold!" (Prov. 16:16 ESV).

But attaining wisdom isn't the only thing you must do to be prepared for your vocation.

Cultivate Character (Who You Are)

Character is vital. People who have developed character fall back on moral "muscle memory" to guide them through difficult decisions. In fact, as British novelist Iris Murdoch once said, "At crucial moments of choice, most of the business of choosing is already over."[6] As you are, so you choose. But being responsible rarely begins the day you take a new job. The battlefield for big responsibilities is the million small tasks you face from childhood onward (Luke 16:10).

A good guide for the character you'll need at work is the second table of God's law, which tells us how to love our neighbor.[7] Of course, a right response to the law's first table—our duty directly to God—is also vital. But the last six commandments are especially applicable to your vocational life as they "contain our duty to man" as concrete expressions of our love for God.[8]

Respect Authority

The fifth commandment—"Honour thy father and thy mother" (Ex. 20:12)—can lead workers "to a greater willingness and cheerfulness in performing their duties to their superiors, as to their parents."[9] Good workers typically learn young to gladly receive correction. Apollos is a good example of a submissive spirit. Well-educated, eloquent, and popular, he was once corrected by Priscilla and Aquila, ordinary artisans. But as a person of good character, he was sensitive to moral authority no matter its earthly voice (Acts 18:24–26; see 2 Pet. 2:16).

Respect Life

The sixth commandment forbids murder. In the words of the Heidelberg Catechism, it also requires us to "love our neighbor as ourselves, to show patience, peace, meekness, mercy, and kindness towards him, and, so far as we have power, to prevent his hurt; also to do good even unto our enemies."[10] Work is not simply about performing a task; it is about promoting life. So you should take into your callings a reverence for human life and a resolve to align your vocational aspirations with God's design for human flourishing. This may mean that if you work in the medical field your bedside manner—the giving of meaningful time and genuine kindness—is as vital as the actual medical care offered. As a checkout clerk your warm smile and thoughtful comments might be more valuable to customers than the items they purchase.

Respect Sexuality

The relational dimensions of the fall warned against in the seventh commandment have poisoned work. From obscene jokes and inappropriate workplace romances, to sexual discrimination and carelessness about how certain businesses facilitate sex trafficking, to outright sexual abuse and the promotion of unbiblical sexual preferences, worksites can be dangerous places. Workers who honor God detest sexual sin and bring to their vocations a desire to preserve chastity in themselves and their coworkers.

Respect Ownership

The eighth commandment, by forbidding theft, requires "a lawful calling, and diligence in it." As a vaccine against the temptation to steal, God requires "an endeavor, by all just and lawful means, to procure, preserve, and further...wealth" (see Eph. 4:28).[11] The commandment also demands honesty at work. The overly ambitious employ "wicked tricks and devices...to draw to [themselves their] neighbor's goods," in the words of the Heidelberg Catechism.[12] Scripture expressly forbids workplace embezzlement, taking for yourself money or goods that have been entrusted to you by an employer (Titus 2:10). God values personal and corporate ownership. So must you.

Respect Truth

Apparently one of the few requirements for today's workers is to simply show up as promised. Those who are disciplined by the ninth commandment—which forbids false testimony—are already better positioned than their peers to truly succeed at work; they fully show up.

Loving and speaking the truth candidly will not always work to your immediate advantage. But God requires it. And a commitment to truth is one of the best ways to witness to the God of truth.

Respect Providence

You will never be satisfied at work if you set your heart on the praise of your colleagues, the defeat of competitors, and the top pay grade. The tenth commandment, in forbidding covetousness, requires "a full contentment with our own condition" and "a charitable frame of the whole soul toward our neighbor."[13] To be happy you don't need a perfect job or ideal coworkers; you need to trust in God's providence, confident that God is working out a good plan for your life.

As you learn to honor the law's second table, you will begin to cultivate character. My friend Andrew told me this: "My job presents challenges around ethical matters—honesty, integrity, truthfulness, fairness." That will be true for you too. So "vocation... necessitates clarity and conviction coupled with empathy and compassion."[14] That's what the second table of the law requires: convictional love. These commandments are light to your path. They put flesh on your basic responsibility to love your neighbor as yourself.

But being equipped with wisdom and character still isn't enough.

Develop Skills (What You Do)

Christian vocation is far more than bringing biblical ideas or even Christian convictions to work. These must be matched by skills that translate who you are and what you know into excellent work, what you do. Throughout the Bible God extols skillfulness. The tabernacle and temple were built by "skilled workers" (2 Chron. 2:7 ESV; see Ex. 35:33). Ezra "was a scribe skilled in the

Law of Moses" (Ezra 7:6 ESV). The virtuous woman of Proverbs 31 had skills that ran both deep and wide. Some people show up to work to get a paycheck. But biblical workers come to perform their craft with excellence.

And while skill is different than attitude, there is a connection between the two. Author and professor Cal Newport contrasts two different mindsets for gaining rewarding work. One focuses "on what the world can offer you." The other cares more for "what you can offer the world."[15] And what you can offer the world in the service of your neighbor are real, tangible, carefully honed, and useful skills. Newport puts it bluntly: "If you want a great job, you need something of great value to offer in return."[16]

This idea can feel daunting. You mean I must master a skill— or even several skills—before I can become useful at work? Not exactly. In fact, even the most well trained have only begun to hone their crafts. By the time you graduate high school or even college it is difficult to be a real expert in anything. But skills can be developed. This is implied in Luke's statement that Jesus grew in stature (2:52). Jesus learned to do better work. Dorothy Sayers writes, "No crooked legs or ill-fitting drawers ever, I dare swear, came out of the carpenter's shop at Nazareth."[17] Surely that was even more true at the end than at the beginning of his tenure as a craftsman.

The younger you are, the more important it is to develop *broad* competence; specialization will come later. Some skills are required no matter the field. Let's consider four examples.

1. **Learn to speak well.** Like God, the most effective workers are good communicators. Take every noble opportunity to practice speaking, especially in front of groups. Because this is one thing most people studiously avoid, learning to speak well can be a huge advantage in almost any field.
2. **Learn to solve problems.** Work is an adventure in problem-solving! I think this is a saving grace of hard math for most students. I doubt I've ever used trigonometry since

finishing the tenth grade. But I'm sure the challenge of the class was beneficial in requiring me to not give up on hard problems.

3. **Learn to work with a team.** We have a romantic interest in the lone hero, the self-made independent person. But when it comes to work, that persona is almost always unwelcome; "organizations by their very nature are social entities where cooperation, collaboration, and coordination are essential capacities."[18] If you do not learn to work with others you will find yourself unemployed; worse, if you are successful you will become a tyrant.

4. **Develop manual or mechanical skills.** We have overstressed the distinction between white- and blue-collar competencies. It is untrue that manual workers don't have to think. It is also false that so-called "knowledge workers" need not work with their hands. In contrast to philosophically oriented cultures, the "Judeo-Christian religious and spiritual tradition is marked by a high affirmation and celebration of the practical arts—the work of the artisan, the craftsperson, the farmer, the work of our hands," like the Proverbs 31 woman.[19] To work with our hands is Godlike (Ps. 19:1). You might not end up in manual labor, but being unhandy is no advantage to anyone.

There are many more skills you need to develop; you'll figure out which ones by talking with your parents and trusted peers. But no matter the skills, they must be developed diligently. The best workers don't simply try hard; they employ what researchers call "deliberate practice,"[20] the application of sustained energy to areas of weakness to rigorously improve a skill. Most of us could never become proficient at a musical instrument through haphazard and irregular practice. Serious exercise is required. Likewise, if you need to improve in math you might need to spend a few hours a day tediously mastering the problems that trouble you. People who develop valuable skills *willingly* get uncomfortable to get better; athletes are one biblical example (1 Cor. 9:24–25). And Paul applies the discipline of an athlete to other vocations, even the pastorate: "I discipline my body and keep it under control" (v. 27 ESV). A commitment to discipline is how you develop skills that will help you in any endeavor.

To live vocationally you must be a Christian, a new creature raised with Christ through the Spirit's effectual call. But deep wisdom, Christlike character, and sought-after skills are not automatically dispensed at conversion. Fearing God is the *start* of a lifelong calling to get wisdom (Ps. 111:10). In terms of character even Jesus grew in "stature, and in favour with God and men" (Luke 2:52). And for most of us skills must be developed with patient diligence. Right now you are in a season of preparation, sowing seeds whose plants you will harvest later (Prov. 20:4). You are developing work habits, social habits, and stewardship habits. It might not seem like much is happening from day to day. But how you live now will add up to what you will bring to your callings later.

British preacher Alexander Maclaren's comment is ominous but true: "The mystic significance of the trivialities of life is that in them we largely make destiny, and that in them we wholly make character."[21] The time to make your character is now: "Life, and nature, and God's law" often "demand that the duty shall be done in its season or left undone forever."[22] To use the language of Ecclesiastes, if you miss the time to plant, keep, and seek, those seasons might not come around again (3:2, 6). You need to have something to offer—not to gain standing with God; Christ offered on the cross means that the Father is well-pleased with every believer. But you must be useful in the world. Through the equipping of the gospel, hear your call: prepare to have something to offer.

John ▶▶▶ *Construction Company CEO*

John founded and managed for decades a successful concrete construction company with over one hundred employees. Even as CEO he demonstrated the kind of flexibility required for a business to succeed; as he says, during those years he could have been found doing many different things, from "operating a shovel to leading meetings on leadership."

John's love of industry began young. He started working on a dairy farm at age eight under the mentorship of a man who was "disciplined, bold, self-motivated, confident, a hard worker, and a Christian." John says he soon realized that he loved the physical demands of farming and "seeing the results of my labor."

John felt that his lack of good grades in high school and his preference for outside work—"dirty and physical"—was steering him in the direction of a trade. Even though John's father, who was also a construction worker, died when he was six, he felt inclined to follow in his father's path.

Principles that John learned over his career include the importance of motivating people to work productively, honoring commitments, and remembering that people are always watching to see if you will live up to your Christian profession. Service in the U.S. Army also taught John disciplines like respect for the chain of command and servant leadership.

Here is John's advice for those showing up to a job interview: "The first impression will tell me a lot. When I first meet [interviewees] I like to shake their hand. A strong, firm grip goes a long way. Can you look me in the eyes when speaking to me? Even their posture matters. I am looking for someone who will stand up tall and straight."

$$\left(\begin{array}{c}5\end{array}\right)$$

CHOOSE WISELY

Choosing can be scary. Especially when it comes to the matter of what you will do with the rest of your life. You've heard older people complain about their work. Some hate what they do. You don't want to end up like them. And you have so many choices. Doubtless there are good vocational options that you don't even know about! Where do you start?

Deciding on a career can be challenging. But don't be intimidated. You can have a heavenly perspective when making hard choices. You cannot map out your life, but you don't have to; you are in God's care. Believers "choose and discern in light of today, and we know the rest of our lives will be lived out one day at a time, one step at a time."[1] God is faithful. He regularly redeems poor human choices.

Still, you must choose. God made human will "with that natural liberty, that is neither forced, nor...determined."[2] Even in a state of grace you won't always choose well. But you must try. And given the relative freedom God has given so many of us today concerning our future work lives, it makes sense to seek a vocation that honors our skills, interests, and potential, so that we can be useful in the world. The older Reformed writers seldom made much of vocational choice; they lived in a time when personal freedom was a small factor in one's vocational future. For you, that factor is greater. So you must choose wisely.

Finding your vocational sweet spot requires several specific actions.

Be Well-Informed

You need to understand your options and what you may be good at, all the while listening to trusted voices.

Know Your Options

A twelfth-century blacksmith's son had no need to inquire about how to become a doctor, lawyer, or farmer. He would most likely become a blacksmith, a noble calling. But in today's world school guidance counselors and curated employment lists might offer surprising insights about future careers. A sales manager for a technology company told me that he attended a job fair that gave him "a great overview of what was available in technology sales. I accepted an offer at that job fair and have stayed in that field for the past twenty-five years." Keep in mind that new fields of employment are constantly developing, so it is wise to also consider up-and-coming occupational opportunities.

Know Yourself

This is a good rule of thumb: "Other things being equal, that calling should be chosen which is most in harmony both with talents and inclination."[3] The Heidelberg Catechism instructs God's people to "feel [themselves] bound to use [their] gifts, readily and cheerfully, for the advantage and welfare of other members."[4] So, you must know what you do well, and that's not easy. In fact, one of the greatest hurdles to sound vocational choice is "the failure to know oneself: the inability to see oneself truthfully...no illusions, no lies, no pretention or facades."[5]

How God has designed you says something about the kind of work you might do well. One of my brothers is a strong and talented mechanic; his grand hands were not made for typing on a small keyboard but for turning large wrenches, which he does expertly. As another example, the disciple Apollos was "an eloquent man" (Acts 18:24); it made sense for him to use his logic and rhetoric to "greatly [help] those who through grace had believed" (v. 27 ESV). He might have been useless working in a shop. There is something special about your combination of talent and training. Your gifts are a sacred trust from God to help others glorify and enjoy him. Hear Paul's pronouncement and ponder how you might put it into practice: "Having then gifts differing according to the grace that is given to us...let us [exercise them] according to the proportion of faith" (Rom. 12:6).

One of the best ways of discovering gifts is often old-fashioned practice. Paul told Timothy to "stir up the gift of God" (2 Tim. 1:6). Fulfilling your duties in small responsibilities can help you figure out where to point your gifts vocationally.

Listen to Others

A wise man once said, "A wise man listens to advice" (Prov. 12:15 ESV). There is wisdom in listening to others because they may be able to help you see talents you don't notice. Or they might calm your passion for an impractical vocation. The reality is, as theologian and professor Gordon Smith observes,

> We each have a remarkable capacity for self-deception. We cannot simply presume that every impression, every longing, ambition, or aspiration is from God. Our longings, fears, and inclinations need the check and confirmation that comes from gracious and frank conversations with those who know us well, will not flatter us, will speak truth to us, and will call us to account.[6]

As the whole church is involved in the choice of a minister (Acts 15:22), so at least *some* church people should be involved in your career choice. Ideally, you'll find a mentor who knows you and something about the field you are considering. If so, watch and listen carefully. Booker T. Washington was right; no education "is equal to that which can be gotten from contact with great men and women."[7] And you have them in your congregation! Be open to suggestions even if you feel certain you already know what you want or don't want to do. After all, notes William Perkins, as "many men are partial in judging their inclinations and gifts, the best way for them is to use the advice and help of others who are able to give direction herein and discern better than they."[8] The way you might best serve others is sometimes hidden to you but clear to others.

The advice of others will not always be perfect, and it will always be shaded by their own experiences. My friend Andrew told me, "My father encouraged me to apply for an office job. He had been a labourer and mechanic and felt that office work offered security." Maybe his father was right. Maybe not. But this advice spurred my friend toward a rewarding vocation as a commercial insurance broker.

Given the vocational freedom we have today, you should begin by evaluating yourself and the fields that might become your life-long occupation with the input of trusted advisors, committing the matter to God in prayer.

Aim High

In the old days the word *ambition* was negative; it suggested a burning desire for fame or power. And this kind of ambition must be avoided in the search for a calling. It is a terrible mistake to choose a vocation out of a desire to be rich or famous. You should never "trust in uncertain riches" (1 Tim. 6:17; see v. 10) or "the praise of men" (John 12:43).

Still, *proper* ambition does have a role to play in selecting an occupation. You should choose the best vocation possible. Of course, God hasn't released a power ranking of human jobs. All legitimate work is good. No one kind of worker has greater value before the Lord. But some callings allow us to do more good than others.

Jesus' parable of the talents suggests that we must leverage our opportunities for the best results for God's kingdom. "We are free," writes Dee Grimes, "to pursue that area of service that is most beneficial to family, church, and commonwealth, and most glorifying to God."[9] We will all have to "give an account of [our] stewardship" (Luke 16:2). And to whom much has been given, from him much is expected (12:48). So responsibilities depend to some degree on your abilities. You must ambitiously apply your unique talents to the providential opportunities you are afforded. You are sowing what you will reap, and you are working in God's vineyard. To be timid or doubtful—refusing to make a potentially helpful proposal at work out of fear of rejection or declining a suitable promotion because of the extra responsibilities entailed—is to squander the Master's gifts. Like Jabez, we should desire enlarged borders within which to do God's work (1 Chron. 4:10).

Scripture actually encourages us to prioritize and select from many good options. We must "earnestly desire the best gifts" (1 Cor. 12:31 NKJV). Commenting on this passage, Calvin says Christians must "apply themselves the more diligently to those things which are most conducive to edification." For Calvin, being a magistrate or politician was "by far the most honorable of all callings in the whole life of mortal man."[10] You might have a hard time agreeing with that! But appreciate Calvin's logic; he lauded the magistracy because it has the potential to wield great influence for Jesus. Not everyone should hold political office. Really. But everyone should prioritize those gifts that have the potential for greater return on investment for the kingdom. Puritan John Cotton argues that an ideal vocation is "fitted to me and my best gifts. For God...would have his best gifts improved to the best advantage."[11]

If possible, you should seek a vocation that allows you to freely imitate God both by expressing creativity and by doing work that has substantial value. Not surprisingly, satisfying work tends to have three traits in common: creativity, impact, and control.[12]

Ideally, future employers will honor your God-given eagerness to perform creative and meaningful work and will allow much freedom to do so. With this in mind, try to discern where you might flourish best and then aim high!

But you also need to be practical.

Be Realistic

You must balance your ideals with providence—including personal limitations and actual opportunities. As one shouldn't commence building a tower without counting the cost (Luke 14:28–30), so you shouldn't embark on a career course without evaluating its potential for success. You may want to be a professor of anthropology. But with high underemployment rates in the field, it might not be a good fit. Some fields, like word processing and typing, used to be in demand but are currently declining at a rapid pace. What you want to do might not be able to provide for yourself or your future family. My friend Karel wanted to be a surgeon and had begun training in that field. But, he says, "I needed bread on the table and gas to fill the tank." So he took a job in a fine hotel restaurant, a position in keeping with his family background. Incidentally, this job prepared Karel to start a very successful bakery that satisfied customers for sixty years.

We have been nurtured to believe in limitless human potential. But in our quest for a calling, as Gordon Smith points out, "We are not looking for perfection; we are looking for a high enough degree of congruence such that we can be effective—giving of our time and energy, knowing that with the investment of our talent and resolve, we are contributing to something bigger than ourselves."[13] So some of us need to be more ambitious; others need to be more reasonable.

Often reasonableness requires rejecting the popular career advice, Just follow your passion. Many people, writes Cal Newport, think that "the key to occupational happiness is to first figure out what you're passionate about and then find a job that matches this passion."[14] And Scripture certainly links joy to work (Deut. 16:15; Eccl. 2:24; 5:19; Heb. 13:17). It hardly seems wise to choose work that gives you no joy. But there are numerous problems with the "passion hypothesis": having clearly defined and vocationally practical passions are rare, they take time to develop, and they tend to be side effects of mastery.[15] In other words, most of us can't know the kind of work we will love until years into the job. Trust me, when I was in high school the last thing I thought I would enjoy was writing and public speaking. But two decades into this calling I can't imagine doing anything else. If we all followed the passions of our youth, much work would be overlooked, and much over-sought. We would all be either firefighters, baseball players, ballerinas, or artists! Aspiration and passion can be one factor in your choice of a career, but not usually a driving force.

Even the more spiritual-sounding suggestion—that you should strive to fulfill *the single* purpose for which God has made you and placed you in his world—can be misleading. God knows what he has in store for us. But he doesn't always reveal his secrets to us. And we needn't try to find them out. We just need to be faithful with what we know (Deut. 29:29).

It has been suggested that "the kind of work we like" indicates "the kind of work we were created to do."[16] And surely working near the intersection of passion and practicality is ideal. But after the fall, vocation is about service. Even in our callings "it is more blessed to give than to receive" (Acts 20:35). On the other hand, relentless dream-chasing naturally feeds selfishness and alienation, especially in "successful" people. The famous author Ernest Hemingway, for example, chased his dreams as a writer, sportsman, and socialite at great cost. He failed to practice sacrificial love, the heartfelt interest in other people that requires abandoning some dreams in order to deeply share in the joy and sadness of more meaningful pursuits. In a documentary, his gray-haired third son chokes up telling the camera that he just wanted his father to love him.[17] Hemingway pursued his passions but came up short in the greatest callings in life.[18] Calvin isn't wrong to call "self-interest... the pestilence that most effectively leads to our destruction."[19]

You don't have to start out, or even end up, absolutely loving what you do. As a Christian, you are not looking for fulfillment at work—you've found it in Christ. Your vocation isn't how you will find yourself—you've found yourself in Jesus.

Still, being realistic doesn't require shelving your creative passions or despising "impractical" professions. It's true that some callings meet the wants, rather than needs, of ourselves and others. But that fact doesn't necessarily make them less valuable. Calvin reminds us that "the invention of arts, and of other things which serve to the common use and convenience of life, is a gift of God by no means to be despised, and a faculty worthy of commendation."[20] Inventions such as the harp "may minister to our pleasure, rather than to our necessity, still it is not to be thought altogether superfluous; much less does it deserve to be condemned."[21] And yet for harp playing to be a viable vocation, someone has to pay you for it. Economic reality requires realistic responses. What you desperately want to do for a career may be better suited for a side job or a hobby.

Dan Doriani sums up these first three points: "When you seek God's call, look with informed discernment for a match between the *internal call* (what you *want* to do) and the *external call* (what an employer is willing to hire you to do)."[22] And even when stubborn facts require you to change direction, thank God that you have options, something the world's majority population knows almost nothing about.

Trust God

There's at least one more vital component to choosing well: trusting God.

When I was in my teens, I had a poor view of God's providence; to me it was something closer to cruel fate. When I faced major decisions, I was sure that only one option was right and that

I would certainly make the wrong choice. With a fatalistic view of the future, making the right decision is like finding the single needle in a vast haystack.

But God's providence isn't like that. There isn't one perfect job that you must magically find. Any number of vocations could be satisfying, provide for those dear to you, and glorify God. You might be truly gifted to flourish in any number of places. You are free to choose any valid calling. For a Christian there are far more right options than wrong ones! No matter what job you end up with, one of the most basic blessings in vocation is that God directs you to a calling and does not permit "you to live an idle, useless and sinful life."[23]

In fact, it is possible to wrongly exaggerate our choice and minimize God's sovereignty. Sometimes he confronts us with callings whether we want them or not: think about Esther or Jonah. God gives assignments in particular roles and places (1 Cor. 7:17). Here's how William Perkins explained it:

> God has determined what He will do with every man...He has in His eternal counsel assigned every man his office and condition of life...He separates every man from the very womb to one calling or other. And accordingly He calls them in time by giving them gifts and will to do that for which they were appointed.[24]

God does all of this. His providence puts you in a place to be faithful.

This means that you might not immediately find what you believe you were called to do. With realistic hopefulness you should seek appealing work, eager to obey God's will. Such an attitude can protect you from the paralysis often caused by the vast number of modern vocational choices and immunize you against the modern passion for keeping options open. Make a decision trusting that God is sovereign even in our vocational choices. A biblical doctrine of providence is a great relief, as Douglas Schuurman explains:

God's providence provides comfort by leading us to the humble self-understanding that as finite, limited beings God calls us only to do our part, at this time and in this place. If God's providence can triumph over the evil actions of Joseph's brothers to save the world from a famine, it can certainly prevail over mistakes and sins we make as we prayerfully discern our callings.[25]

God's sovereignty can help us accept callings we suspect will be hard—bearing and raising children, managing the family business, taking a lower-paying job to be near a faithful church. So, as Perkins writes, "He who has gifts fit for his place, and is in good manner called thereto by them whose duty it is to call, may assure himself that he is called by God."[26]

Because of God's covenantal faithfulness you can prayerfully choose but leave the results to the Lord. Perkins understood the anxiety we often experience when we think about work: "Men commonly take upon them a double care: one is to do the works and labors of their callings; [and] the other is to procure a blessing and good success to their foresaid labors."[27] But you don't have to worry about success. Leave that to God. In fact, notes Paul Helm, "identifying *one* particular job or profession or task with God's will...[is] a kind of idolatry...since all lawful human interests are in accordance with God's will."[28] Moreover, as theologian Herman Hanko writes, through vocation God "gives an assignment in the kingdom that is exactly right according to the abilities which he knows" his children possess.[29] God will not mislead you.

In his *Doctrine of the Christian Life*, theologian John Frame gives a helpful definition of vocation; he emphasizes the work that God is doing in our lives. Frame says that a vocation is the aligning of the gifts God has given us, the Spirit's guidance through self-examination and the input of other believers, providential opportunities, and divine assistance in wisely practicing our gifts.[30]

You must choose a vocation. But you can trust that "God's callings are discerned quietly, when the heart of faith joins opportunities and gifts with the needs of others."[31] Care about the needs of your neighbors. Seek opportunities. Be committed to using your gifts. Practice faith in Christ whose righteousness gives you the freedom to work for the good of your neighbor. And trust that behind your choices is the ever-faithful working of a loving God.

Tim ►►► *Philosophy Professor*

Tim teaches philosophy at a state university. From his mid-teens he knew he wanted to work in education, but it wasn't always obvious which discipline he should pursue. He says of his younger self, "I had great anxiety about speaking in front of groups of people." That's not ideal for a college professor!

But Tim had grit. And his early work as a dishwasher taught him the importance of honoring commitments. "One crazy night there were only two of us washing dishes as the restaurant hosted a large banquet," he says. "As carts of dishes lined up far faster than the two of us could wash, my partner grew agitated and quit. I stayed until deep into the night, scraping charred mustard out of large vats and cycling endless stacks of plates through the dishwasher. I think I was fifteen. But I knew I had made a commitment to do a job and had to keep my word."

Finding out what we don't want to do for a living is often easy. Even then, it is usually wise to follow the adage: Get a job and keep it until you get a better one. To determine how your talents might pair with meaningful work, Tim recommends finding "wise, honest, experienced people who know you well and are willing to tell you what you're cut out for. There will be a set of skills to develop; start early and work steadily to acquire them. Accept from the outset that your career path isn't necessarily going to be a straight one. Do well whatever job you have for the time being."

Not all work is equally stimulating. Tim gives the example of a hardware store worker: "Nails and paint may not be intrinsically rewarding. But learning how to help people do useful things is itself good, and it may open doors for conversations and friendships that have value far transcending mundane home repairs."

6

REMEMBER YOUR
OTHER VOCATIONS

I t is tempting to think about *vocation* as if it were synonymous with *occupation*. And it is true that our work lives matter profoundly. Most people spend much of the waking hours of the middle portion of their lives working. The substantial weight of your work life on the "scale" of who you are means that if you aren't godly at work then you aren't godly at all.

But one's work life is not sovereign. Paul Helm writes that "for the Christian...there is not one supreme duty which he has to fulfill but there are numerous competing duties and interwoven relationships each of which claims time, energy and commitment."[1] You must work to the glory of God. But you won't do "all to the glory of God" if you fail to respect your other vocations (1 Cor. 10:31).

In the introduction to his Small Catechism, Martin Luther identifies key Scripture texts that give instruction for what he calls "holy orders," or the various "estates" in which God's people must live out "their office and duty."[2] Luther was convinced of the sacredness of "everyday activities in the workplace, the culture, the church, and especially the family."[3] Luther was right; you must be a worker. But no matter your occupation, you must also glorify God in the family and in the church. And in every vocation, your gender calling as male or female must exert a significant influence—an influence that is often minimized in our egalitarian culture.

Gender

A booklet published by the Reformed Presbyterian Church of North America addressing gender confusion is aptly titled *Gender as Calling*. The booklet insists that "humans are created by God with one or the other anatomical sex, and that sexual identity marks that person's gender calling."[4] You are a man or a woman. That fact is grounded in creation. You can't choose it. You can't change it. God has already decided for you. And God's choice of your gender influences how you are to serve him. Gender "is both an anatomical identity and a social calling...To be sexually male is also to be socially male, and likewise for the female."[5] We mustn't embrace non-biblical cultural stereotypes—that only women change diapers, and men should only do outdoor work at home. Much less may we condone sinful discrimination, preventing a man or woman to perform a task that Scripture doesn't keep them from. Still, we may never allow our vocational zeal to eclipse our gender.

Biologists can identify numerous differences between men and women beyond obvious physiology—this would not have surprised almost anyone throughout history. Men and women are different so that they can complement each other, filling out together what it means to image God. Author and speaker Nancy Pearcey points out that

> even though most virtues are universally human—both men and women are called to be loving, merciful, just, courageous, and so on—those virtues may be exercised differently in male versus female experience. Our goal should not be to deny those differences but to be grateful for the unique contribution of each of the sexes.[6]

Gender differences offer practical advantages. For example, they "[enhance] pair bonding"—sparking and deepening godly interest between a man and a woman—"dual parenting, and extensive division of labor."[7] And our differences affect our responsibilities. Rosaria Butterfield reminds us that "because our creational design is different, some aspects of obedience to God are different."[8] The first man was to work the ground. The first woman was to raise children (Gen. 3:16–19). These roles aren't exclusive to either gender—men also raise children, and women also toil. But all our callings, including occupations, are influenced by gender. In the most unifying of all relationships, marriage, spouses have different callings. Wives are to submit to their own husbands, and husbands are to love their wives as Christ loves the church (Eph. 5:22, 25). Even outside of marriage the Bible outlines unique gender roles. In general, as pastor John Piper observes, men "lead, provide for, and protect," often taking risks to do so. Women "affirm, receive and nurture strength and leadership," and often have a greater capacity for patience and moderation.[9]

Especially today women need to reject the cultural pressures to try to be like men. The irony of feminism is that many modern women "have modeled themselves on the very men they have criticized."[10] But Scripture urges women to rejoice in the high calling of femininity. Whether at work or at home, the world needs women to fulfill their vocation to be women. Like our Lord's godly mother (Luke 1:38), women cheerfully receive the Lord's will, testifying against a world bent on asserting. And into the frenzied, confused mess of sinful people, true femininity breathes the life-giving power "of a gentle and quiet spirit" (1 Pet. 3:4 ESV). Godly women respectfully decline the aggressive race-to-the-top mentality that consumes so many others; something men also must resist.

Women may work outside of the home (see Prov. 31:14, 24). But if they marry and raise children and spend most of their time in the home, they choose a high and happy calling (Ps. 113:9). Some women can do both well. Many mothers effectively pursue vocations that allow them to work part-time or work from home. But, whatever the case, when godly mothers learn to view motherhood as their first and primary vocation and then wisely integrate their other vocations, they will, as one Christian woman notes, "have profound influence" on young people.[11]

Toward that end, it is a great calling of older women to "teach the young women to be sober, to love their husbands, to love their children, to be discreet, chaste, keepers at home, good, obedient to their own husbands" (Titus 2:4–5). When they do these things, they actually protect the reputation of God's word and are excellent examples of godliness in a wicked world. A woman's place is not restricted to the home. But women, along with men, need to recognize their limitations: "Some women are frustrated because they think they can and should be the best homemaker, the best mother and wife, and the very best in their profession—all at the same time."[12] Wisdom knows its limits. And the thoughtful mother will not count it a loss to lay down career goals in order to take up the calling to raise children for God—especially as she remembers that changing seasons of life may present her with opportunities to pursue many God-honoring vocational goals (see Proverbs 31).

For their part men should take it not as a burden but as a God-ordained privilege to labor—physically and mentally, without complaining, and without demanding praise and approval. God has called them to imitate Jesus the Good Shepherd in sacrificially leading, defending, and feeding their dependents as well as their neighbors in the broader world, as providence allows.[13]

Never forget that your maleness or femaleness is basic to who you are and must affect how you work.

Family

It is not too strong to say, as Gene Veith and his daughter Mary Moerbe observe, that the family is "the primary estate and the site of our most important earthly vocations. The family is God's ongoing creation of humanity, the foundation of our culture, and the image of our relationship with God on earth."[14] In God's generosity our labor often allows us not only to provide for ourselves and our families but also to contribute to the development and support of society. But you are not responsible for all people equally. John Calvin notes that "the more closely men are bound together by ties of kinship, of acquaintanceship, or of neighborhood, the more responsibilities for one another they share."[15] Our first calling is to family.

And yet there is often tension between our occupational vocations and our family calling. In disobedience to a family calling, some people work too little. This is a great sin. An able person who refuses to "provide...for his own" commits spiritual apostasy (1 Tim. 5:8).

But there is another way to mishandle family and work. The hard worker can neglect the family. And industrialization has made this sin easier to justify. Until the industrial revolution many parents didn't go to work. They did their work at home—the blacksmith in his shed, the farmer in his fields, the watchmaker in the storefront shop beneath his house. In fact, this is why in his introduction to the small catechism Luther failed to even mention work as a calling—in his day the lines between home and job were so blurred that they barely existed. Truly, "the household [is] the fundamental building block for both society and the economy."[16] Especially in agrarian societies, work doesn't prevent parents from discipling their children as they "sit in [the] house...walk by the way...lie down" and rise up (Deut. 6:7 ESV). When people work in or near the home, often alongside their children, there are natural and ample opportunities for fathers and mothers to train their children how to be godly in all of life.

By contrast, modern work forms threaten biblical discipleship. Between commuting and laboring, many workers are away from the home at least nine hours a day. That's not a sin. But it is a challenge. And it is possible for one's commitment to work to *become* sinful. Is it wrong for a man to work forty hours a week? How about sixty? Eighty? One hundred? One hundred twenty? There isn't a biblical work-time-to-family-time ratio. But at some point family becomes the victim of work, not its beneficiary. A man must provide sustenance for his family. But he must also provide counsel and godly example, which require presence. We should work as much as necessary to obey God's command that we "labor, doing honest work with [our] own hands, so that [we] may have something to share with anyone in need" (Eph. 4:28 ESV). And you should begin now to find the right stride; even as an unmarried young adult you should be preparing to work like a family man or woman. Care for those closest to you. Balance your work life with meaningful relationships.

And as you launch out into careers, realize that you are entering the early phase of a shift in parent/child roles. This relationship is dynamic, not static. In God's household parents care for needy children; later, children care for needy parents.[17] Godly children recognize their calling to help their parents in the difficult aging process. They honor parents who are typically becoming more set in their ways. They offer advice where appropriate. They help perform now-difficult tasks. They provide financial support as needed, believing that, as John Frame writes, "Welfare is first of all a family responsibility" (see Matt. 15:3–7; 1 Tim. 5:4, 8).[18] Getting a job does not free a young person from the fifth commandment. Admittedly, many young people beginning to make vocational choices have parents who are fully capable of independent living. Still, your early vocational choices can have long-term implications.

Twentieth-century philosopher, musician, and physician Albert Schweitzer was known to criticize people who constantly looked to do something extraordinary but took little notice for their ordinary responsibilities: "Such persons wanted to dedicate themselves to larger tasks because those that lay nearest did not satisfy them."[19] In your quest for satisfying work you can easily neglect family. You must not.

Church

Believers in Christ are, according to the Heidelberg Catechism, "living [members]" of the community Christ has chosen for eternal life.[20] We don't create this community; we are effectually called into it. But when God calls us into his body, he gives us a church vocation where responsibilities flow from privileges. Luther asked, "When do we use the doctrine of the Church properly?" Not only must we "be and remain members of the invisible Church by sincere faith in the Redeemer." But we must also "adhere to the Church which teaches the Word of God in all its purity" and "do all in our power to maintain, promote, and extend this Church by prayer, personal service, and financial support."[21]

This calling is sacred and cannot be compromised by your occupation. In fact, the church is meant to be the vocation that equips you for your other callings; in it Christ communicates to us the benefits of redemption through the means of grace. Preaching and the sacraments reveal Christ, unite us to him, and strengthen our faith in him. Regular worship provides an essential rhythm to our lives; fellowship with God's people encourages us to be faithful. So, it is true, as Donald Heiges observes, that "unless Christians take their calling seriously within the church there is not much hope of their taking it seriously in the world."[22]

When considering an occupation, you should ask questions concerning your calling as a church member. If the job requires a move, is there a faithful church that you could join? Will your shifts be conducive to regular Lord's day worship? No job should be so enticing that you would consider slighting the role Christ intends the church to play in your life. Concerning the church, the Belgic Confession teaches that no one "ought to withdraw himself to live in a separate state from it." This is true regardless of your "status or condition,"[23] or your aspiration for further education or a promising occupation.

Some jobs don't require a move, but they might make demands

that could be dangerous to your spiritual life by limiting your adherence to the church. Some jobs will keep you from the means of grace God offers in the church. Many professing Christians consider regular church attendance to be incidental to their spiritual well-being. But God requires his people to "diligently attend church," as the Heidelberg Catechism puts it. And for good reason: "to learn what God's Word teaches, to participate in the sacraments, to pray to the Lord publicly, and to bring Christian offerings for the poor."[24] We must not neglect "to meet together, as is the habit of some" (Heb. 10:25 ESV). Your spiritual health depends on gathering.

Of course, there are legitimate reasons for Christians to work on the Lord's day. Some jobs truly embody "works of necessity and mercy" that are not forbidden on the Lord's day.[25] But that is not to say that choosing even a worthy career that competes with congregational worship will be good for your soul. Something may be lawful but not helpful (1 Cor. 6:12; 10:23). The fourth commandment is both a law and a gift. The Westminster Larger Catechism gets at both aspects. God sanctifies Sunday as a day for his service and ordains it to be a means to bless us "*in* our sanctifying [of] it."[26] One of the ways we sanctify the Lord's day is to exercise "such foresight, diligence, and moderation, to dispose and seasonably dispatch our worldly business" during the rest of the week "that we may be the more free and fit for the duties of that day."[27] We should also do this in our choice of a career. Resolve early in your working years to prioritize congregational life and corporate worship so that you can use the Lord's day as God intends it.

And as you think about how to ensure that your occupational calling respects your ecclesiastical calling, take the time to assess your current place in Christ's church. If you are mature enough to be entrusted with responsibilities in the world, the same should be true regarding your church life. Spiritually speaking, are you transitioning to adulthood (1 Cor. 13:11)? Are you both hearing about Christ and trusting in him? Are you both attending worship and actually worshiping God with your heart, soul, mind, and strength? In the church are you "serving to the edification of the brethren," as the Belgic Confession admonishes us?[28] People your age are taking their places in the world's industries and economies. You or your peers will be operating forty-ton tractor trailers, interning in influential communications industries, providing urgent medical care, and going to war. Are you not capable of also serving in the church? Os Guinness is right: "Anyone citing his or her individual calling as grounds for rejecting the church's corporate calling is self-deluded."[29]

You are a whole person made up of body and soul. Your callings should respect both. You are male or female; this means you should work and serve in ways consistent with your divinely-assigned gender. You are a unique individual, but you don't live for yourself (2 Cor. 5:15). You were born into a family and at no time in this present age are you released from family obligations. Your work matters. But so does your worship and service in the church of Christ.

To see your "whole life as a divine 'calling'" is the "cement which holds together the various aspects of our lives, preventing them from splitting up into different, and disjointed, sealed compartments," says Helm.[30] Unless the Lord's calling is the foundation of every part of a person's life, writes Calvin, "there will be no harmony among the several parts of his life. Accordingly, your life will then be best ordered when it is directed to this goal."[31] Commit to being a worker. And don't forget your other vocations.

Penny ▶▶▶ Packaging Production Manager

Penny is a retired manager from a large pharmaceutical company. She chose this job—after much prayer—because it allowed her more time at home with her young children after her husband left the family. She loved her previous job. But "something had to change."

Previously, Penny had a couple of summer jobs during college that especially impacted her life. She reflects on those jobs: "One summer I worked in housekeeping at a hotel. It taught me that no job is beneath me as long as it's honest work. Another summer I worked as a cleanup technician in a hospital surgical unit. There I learned the importance of carefully following instructions and paying attention to detail; someone's life was at stake if those instruments were not cleaned and sanitized correctly." Penny learned her work ethic from her parents; her father was a teacher in an all-black school during the days of segregation, and her mother worked in a factory. From them she learned the importance of responsibility and determination.

In addition to encouraging young people to seek work that aligns with their skills and interests and listening to sound advice from trusted advisors, Penny suggests taking opportunities to shadow someone in a field of interest.

Penny observes that the challenges in her manager position "always centered around integrity. When I traveled for the company, it would have been easy for me to fudge my expense report because I was given a blank check." She insisted on treating all her employees equally, even those who did not like her and were looking for excuses to catch her violating the rules. Penny was able to be faithful by remembering that she did her work unto God.

PART
THREE

PRACTICING
VOCATION

WORK WELL

"Six days shalt thou labour, and do all thy work" (Ex. 20:9). God's ground for this command is simple: "In six days the LORD made heaven and earth, the sea, and all that in them is" (v. 11). We are the image of God. We work because God works.

But Scripture doesn't simply command work; it requires a particular way of working. Living vocationally is more than getting a job and showing up. *How* you work says a lot about who you are and what you really believe about God. You must work "heartily, as to the Lord, and not unto men" (Col. 3:23). You must always abound "in the work of the Lord" (1 Cor. 15:58).

Here's the problem: many professing Christians deny that the believer must "do excellent work in an effort to bring glory to God."[1] Troublingly, they are apparently content to perform mediocre work, just enough to get by. Many Christians fail to realize that their labors should "adorn the doctrine of God our Savior" (Titus 2:10). Your work habits can either validate or undermine your claim of faith and repentance.

John the Baptist exhorted those who came to be baptized to bear "fruits worthy of repentance" (Luke 3:8). And he applied such a life to our vocations. Of those who asked John how to bear penitent fruit, some were tax collectors and soldiers. John told them how to work as evidence of their new life with God (vv. 10–14). It

FINDING MY VOCATION

is not too much to say, after all, that vocation is "the main arena in which we practice faith, repentance, and new obedience."² John's clinic on the intersection of faith and work lays a solid foundation for God-honoring vocational habits.

Be Responsible

The question asked by the tax collectors and soldiers implies that they, the workers, bore the brunt of the responsibility to work well. "What shall we do?" (Luke 3:12, 14). Personalize that question: How must *I* work? Even in the most micro-managed work environment you are ultimately responsible for your performance. And this is so because you are responsible to God for how you work. Responsible people understand that God has appointed them to his service (1 Tim. 1:12), that their work matters, that with God's help they can do the work that has been assigned to them, and that one day they will have to give account to God for all their works (Eccl. 12:14). We become the people God made us to be by taking up the work he has called us to do, all in the context of sovereign saving grace. Truly, "responsibility [is] the key to human identity."³

Our responsibility before God is why Scripture is filled with calls to work well. Paul told the church at Ephesus that even slaves, though lacking freedom, had responsibilities to work obediently, with a sincere heart, "with good will doing service, as to the Lord and not to men" (Eph. 6:5–7). This is the case also for prisoners and other people who have limited employment opportunities. It is unreasonable to tell such people to follow their dreams, and that's not Scripture's message. We must be faithful where God puts us.

You have no excuse for poor vocational performance—a hard boss, difficult coworkers, personal limitations; you are responsible for being faithful to what the Lord asks of you. As Peter puts it, "As each has received a gift, use it to serve one another, as good stewards of God's varied grace" (1 Pet. 4:10 ESV). You are a steward. And "it is required in stewards, that a man be found faithful" (1 Cor. 4:2), whether stewarding one talent or ten, with a hard boss or a gentle

78

one. And many of us have more "graces, blessings, and gifts" than we realize.[4] As the Lord tasked each tribe to fight for its own territory in the land of Canaan, so each of us is called to do our part in God's world. Os Guinness writes that answering our call "by its very nature is stepping forward to responsibility." And "responsibility is obedience by another name."[5] How would it change your attitude if God came to you and said, My child, I would like you to change diapers today. Or, Enter that data for my sake? This is, in fact, happening when God calls us to do "the will of God from the heart; with good will doing service, as to the Lord, and not to men" (Eph. 6:6–7).

Being responsible to God means refusing to work in a fleshly way, compromising our values for the sake of progress, or convenience. A Christian worker, for example, will not massage the numbers on a spreadsheet to make his sales report more appealing or present an AI-developed promotional script as if it were her own work. Instead, you must work like God works, being even vocationally "conformed to the image" of Christ (Rom. 8:29), through "active, functional, daily reliance on the indwelling power of the Holy Spirit." The righteous "practice God's presence in the midst of their labors," says author Amy Sherman.[6] After all, as Luther taught, vocation is God's mask. "God is hidden in vocation, which means that he is present and active, though not perceived, in works and offices of human beings."[7]

Faithfulness in responsibility is the only way to experience God's approval and the respect of our consciences.

Be Productive

Before the tax collectors and soldiers asked John how they could fulfill their vocations to the glory of God, John gave this general exhortation: "Every tree therefore that does not bear good fruit is cut down and thrown into the fire." And he laced this warning with urgency: "Even now the axe is laid to the root of the trees" (Luke 3:9 ESV). Christians must work to be as fruitful as possible. Love your neighbor by producing goods and offering services that will contribute to their flourishing. Work for your superiors as you would have others work for you if the roles were reversed (Matt. 7:12).

Scripture calls you to diligent work: "Whatever your hand finds to do, do it with your might" (Eccl. 9:10 ESV); "Whatever you do, work heartily" (Col. 3:23 ESV). The gospel supplies God's people with divine energy to work hard at every noble task. In our day of efficiency, shortcuts, and life hacks it is easy to overlook the importance of hard work, the kind that grants, in Puritan Richard Steele's words, "inward peace and comfort at night after you have been diligently employed in your calling."[8] But effective people know that there is no replacement for old-fashioned industry; by the grace of God Paul accomplished great things by laboring hard (Acts 20:35; see 1 Thess. 2:9). Faithful workers don't give themselves *to* their work. But they do give themselves *when* they work.

With God's blessing, when diligence and skill combine, the result is a fruitful life. "A man diligent in his business...shall stand before kings" (Prov. 22:29). That is to say, only diligent, skillful work honors God; "work must be good work before it can call itself God's work."[9] Not all Christians believe this. Some undermine what is done by the body since what really matters, they think, is a spiritual life with God. But God calls us to glorify him in the body (1 Cor. 6:20), by the deeds done in the body (2 Cor. 5:10). "No piety in the worker will compensate for work that is not true to itself; for any work that is untrue to its own technique is a living lie," writes Dorothy Sayers.[10] Christian tax collectors honor God by collecting the authorized tax. Christian soldiers honor God by skillfully doing their part to defend their state. Of course, God doesn't need your productivity. The God who could "raise up children unto Abraham" from ordinary stones could get his work done without you (Luke 3:8). But he has chosen you to do his work. So, you must strive to be productive for his kingdom.

Productivity flowing from excellent work is also how we find joy in our work. A person's "satisfaction," writes Sayers, "comes, in the godlike manner, from looking upon what he has made and finding it very good."[11] Contentment in poor work is a sign of a compromised heart.

Be Focused

If we compare John's exhortation to soldiers with one of Paul's illustrations, we will grasp the importance of focus. "No soldier gets entangled in civilian pursuits" (2 Tim. 2:4 ESV)—a soldier drafted for war must set aside his hobbies and leave behind, for a time, even his home and family. Paul's point is that soldiers glorify God by focusing on the specific mission to which they are called. We could generalize Paul's observation: good workers refuse to get entangled in work that is not properly their own. Thus, focus is one of the "indispensable capacities" required for "living well and working well."[12] The reason is simple: as the body is healthy when "each part does its work" (Eph. 4:16 NIV), so a healthy society requires everyone to understand his or her place and fulfill his or her role. Paul puts it simply: "Do your own business" (1 Thess. 4:11).

Sadly, this is not normal. Without a clear aim at what is most important, we are prone to fall back on what is easiest, or most immediately rewarding—as a pastor it might be tempting for me to engage in online theological debates when I should be writing a sermon. A student might prefer to binge-watch videos, perhaps with the justification that they are related to his field of study, instead of doing research for a presentation.

We can also confuse productivity with busyness. But often the more broadly we spread ourselves, the less we actually accomplish. Unless we are busy at the right things, we may miss our callings. Busybodies are "not busy at work" but "walk in idleness" (2 Thess. 3:11 ESV; see 1 Tim. 5:13). They can fill their calendars with tasks but do not occupy themselves in ways that please God. When I worked on a construction crew in my late teens, someone would often shout, "Look busy," when the boss unexpectedly arrived at work. But we shouldn't have tried to *look* busy; we should have *been* busy with the tasks we had been assigned.

This is why valuable producers are "rarely haphazard in their work habits."[13] They know what they should do and develop the disciplines to stay on track. Essentially, vocational focus is simply asking and answering this question, in Cal Newport's words: "What makes sense for me to do with the time that remains?"[14]

Focus is saying a robust yes to what is most central to your mission and saying no to everything else. Not because you are unkind or selfish. But because in God's vast world you have been given a particular field to work. This may mean refusing to use your phone for entertainment or even personal communication when you are on the clock or declining an invitation to attend an interesting but time-consuming conference in a field completely unrelated to your major. Greg McKeown explains that "many capable people are kept from getting to the next level of contribution because they can't let go of the belief that everything is [equally] important."[15] Even Jesus had a laser-focused ministry. He set wise goals and pursued them, refusing to stray (see Luke 12:14). A godly man looks at his work and, says Puritan John Cotton, "if it [appears] to be his calling, faith doth not pick and choose as carnal reason will do."[16]

Focus will make you a better contributor in your callings. It will also help you enjoy your work. When we are unclear about our responsibilities, goals, and roles, we "experience confusion, stress, and frustration."[17]

Be Loving

Jesus reminds us of the primacy of love in the pursuit of any vocation: "Whoever has two tunics is to share with him who has none, and whoever has food is to do likewise" (Luke 3:11 ESV). Love is our primary obligation to our neighbors, whether we find them at home, at play, or at work. Love is the Christian's chief vocation; everything God tells us to do can be summarized by a single word, *love* (Gal. 5:14). The two great commands—to love God and our neighbor (Matt. 22:37–40)—are like a vocational North Star, helping us know whether we are on course.

Commenting on the possibility of an AI takeover, one writer gets to the point of vocation: "There remains one thing that only human beings are able to create and share with one another: love."[18] If you don't love, you fail the test of vocation. If you are excellent at the technical side of your calling, or efficient in the execution of your tasks, or an effective manager of people but have not love, you are nothing (see 1 Cor. 13). Without love, vocation and its potential bestowal of meaning and purpose devolve into a hodgepodge of disjointed tasks. Douglas Schuurman writes that "particular duties are callings or vocations insofar as the vocation or calling to be a Christian is expressed through them."[19] And that calling is to love.

Your work is an opportunity to promote human flourishing, not only by producing goods and rendering services, but by treating people as divine-image bearers. Boaz used his vocation as a farmer to honor God by providing for the poor in a way that preserved their dignity (Ruth 2:8–9). As Boaz realized, love places my neighbors' interests above my own. Lovers heartily believe and rigorously practice the truth that service is better than being served (Acts 20:35). Truly vocational Christians forget about their ego and remember that "some of the most significant work we do is done in obscurity."[20]

In your work you must invest in people. Our incarnate Savior did not merely perform tasks; he entered the lives of his beloved ones. So should we; "the Christian's life, meaning, and purpose will always be shaped by the greatness of God and by the presence we offer others."[21]

Be Content

Even with near record low unemployment creating a workers' market, only 60 percent of workers are currently satisfied. And this is actually an all-time high! Still, that means that nearly half of workers are not content.[22] Many workers think they will only be satisfied with higher pay, greater respect, and more recognizable achievements. A hearty embrace of vocation can change that. So, John tells believing soldiers, "Be content with your wages" (Luke 3:14). He might have added, be content with the whole of the vocation God has given to you. And the command is important. Those who in their work are covetous rather than content show that, as Perkins puts it, "they were never thoroughly touched with any sense or feeling of the need they had of Christ."[23]

We achieve contentment partly by resting in God's providence instead of complaining, despairing, or envying others. John Calvin explains how a right view of vocation can foster contentment. No task will be so troublesome, "provided you obey your calling in it, that it will not shine and be reckoned very precious in God's sight."[24] Not all work is stimulating or immediately rewarding. Some work feels useless. And it is fine to seek more rewarding employment (1 Cor. 7:21). But in the meantime, discouraged but believing workers can know that their works "are pleasing unto God, and that He will give a blessing unto them for Christ's sake," says Perkins.[25] And your work is more important than you realize. Believe it: "By God's grace, we do more good than we know."[26] We don't *only* fix cars, make sales calls, produce reports, cut grass, or drive trucks. We are the hands and feet of God in the service of others.

I frequently pass a homemade plywood yard sign in the shape of a tractor and trailer that says, "If you own it a trucker delivered it." Thank God for truckers! Thank God for mechanics who do an honest job for honest pay. Thank God for landscapers who beautify creation. Thank God for office workers who perform mundane behind-the-scenes tasks that can truly make life better. If you are working hard at a legitimate calling, you are truly "solving the world's problems."[27] The English novelist George Eliot wrote that the "good of the world is partly dependent on unhistoric acts." For our quality of life we should be thankful for those "who lived faithfully a hidden life, and rest in unvisited tombs."[28] No one is a *mere* worker. As Michael Berg puts it,

> All vocations are higher than us. We are lifted up into them. They are divine. It's a privilege to be God's coworker. It's the highest honor. There is no stooping low into a job that is beneath us. All vocations are higher than us.[29]

And vocational contentment can deepen over time. Perseverance often leads to the honing of skills that can cultivate satisfaction and contentment, so don't be quick to change jobs. Beware of vocationally hurrying "hither and thither," as Calvin put it, if "harassed by a continual restlessness."[30] Loyalty to a worthy employer is increasingly rare. And frequent job changes don't look good on a resume. More importantly, short work tenures can cancel the challenging but rewarding pursuit of contentment.

A calling, said Perkins, is like a compass that shows us the direction in which we approach God even in our ordinary labors.[31] And so, while carefully choosing a calling is not insignificant, simply "working right trumps finding the right work."[32] At work—as in your other vocations—you have the opportunity to answer the question, What should this world be like? If you are working well and relying on God to establish the work of your hands for you (Ps. 127:1; 90:17), there is no telling what you might accomplish. In every calling Christians are meant to show to the world the work God is currently doing and preview the coming of God's glory. "The first place believers should look to conduct their foretaste-bringing mission is right at the current job they hold."[33]

Ask Scripture, how should I work? And then do what it says with all your heart.

Walter ▶▶▶ *Graphic Designer and Magazine Editor*

Walter has worked in the publishing industry in New Zealand for over fifty years. Today he is a semi-retired graphic designer and magazine editor. When Walter finished high school, he was uncertain about what to do next. But his mother showed him an advertisement for an apprenticeship at a newspaper, and it appeared that enough of the required skills seemed to fit with his abilities.

Walter wasn't immediately passionate about the work. But he learned to love what he did because he "was serving the Lord in this capacity, and it was worthwhile. It was with purpose."

How did he flourish in this work? He says, "What was most valuable for me was developing a good work ethic, which included how I related to my employer and work colleagues. I also was constantly developing my skills and knowledge of the industry. Even today, after retiring several years ago, I am still working (part time) and still learning." Walter encourages young people to get the best education they can. He adds, "Be prepared to grow in your skills and accept added responsibility if it comes your way."

Like all work, the publishing industry comes with challenges for Christians; Walter had to answer the question, What do you do when asked to design work that runs contrary to your faith? Some jobs may not be suitable for believers. But we must work heartily in the jobs we accept. As Walter says, "Being a Christian, I always strived to conduct my business with integrity, honesty, and transparency. It was important that my clients could trust that I was always giving them my very best. Even after retirement, these clients still want me to work for them."

BE SURE TO REST

For people listening to God's voice, the importance of work is a given. The Bible is a record of God working to redeem a people to work for him. Regardless of our particular callings, divine image-bearers must work as God works. And the fourth commandment presents a proper ratio for work: "Six days shalt thou labour, and do all thy work" (Ex. 20:9). Over 85 percent of your week should be largely occupied by your ordinary labors. You were made to work.

But you weren't made to *only* work. And you won't work well if you are consumed by work: "The seventh day is the sabbath of the LORD thy God: in it thou shalt not do any work." People need rest. So do animals (Ex. 20:10). Even the soil from which we gather food can benefit from occasional breaks (Lev. 25:3–4).

It may be that you love work. And that's what God wants for you (Eccl. 5:19)! But that love needs to be properly stewarded. Especially successful people are tempted to believe that their work is ultimate, that the meaning of their lives consists in production. The fourth commandment, as a summary of God's will for the right ordering of your schedule, challenges that false assumption. To honor God's intention for balanced living, you need a theology of rest that you implement on a daily and weekly basis.

You Need a Theology of Rest

A theology of rest is simple: God "knoweth our frame; he remembereth that we are dust" (Ps. 103:14). God's commandment of rest is a gift. By it God cares for us. After all, as William Perkins puts it, "God, who is the sovereign King over all, might have enjoined us a perpetual labor from one day to another for all the days of our lives. But, tendering our good and salvation, He enjoined us to labor six days, commanding a vacation on the seventh."[1]

Vacation didn't have the same meaning in Perkins' day. Rest, even Sunday rest, isn't time off from responsibility; but it does mean "vacating" the normal cares and burdens of our ordinary callings. It is a testimony to the renewing work that God does in us even apart from our efforts. You are not divine. You cannot flourish without rest. You need time when you are not producing but only receiving, when you are not earning but only trusting.

Sadly, many Christians do not have a proper understanding of the need for this rest because "the texture of [their] Sunday observance is more often than not determined by [customs] that have long since [lost sight of] whatever scriptural basis" they might have.[2] Some Lord's day habits are justified and need to be reinforced by a study of their origin. But others are characterized by either service of one's selfish desires on the one hand or in meticulously following "the commandments of men" (taught as doctrine) on the other (Matt. 15:9).

To understand the importance of regular rest, you need to see the subject in the context of the story of Scripture. In the fourth commandment God grounds the rule of weekly rest in his creation of the world and his rescue of Israel from Egypt. At creation God initiated a rhythm of work and rest. You work because God works. But you don't share God's omnipotence. God didn't *need* to rest from his creative works. You do. You also need a day to remember that the Lord is your salvation, that he has rescued you from spiritual Egypt. Moreover, the Lord's day should bring to your mind the Christian's eternal rest. As Zacharias Ursinus, the author of the Heidelberg Catechism, puts it, "The Sabbath is an image or type of the spiritual rest from sin which the faithful shall enjoy in the life to come."[3]

You can't create that rest. You must receive it. And you can begin to experience it now as you gladly rest from your sins and from trusting in your perceived righteousness. You can't do that as a disembodied spirit—you must set aside real time, on a real day, to practice rest in a world of real toil.[4]

How you balance your work with rest says a lot about your understanding of vocation. In fact, rest is part of your calling. Besides accounting for 14 percent of your life, the Lord's day is meant to be like a pace car, the car that occasionally regulates the speed of the rest of the cars in a race; it can keep you in step with God the rest of your days. It helps calibrate your heart. It manifests your priorities. And it can help shape a lifetime of living before God's face. Rest is one of the clearest ways that you testify to God's sufficiency. In this way, "resting resembles tithing," the deliberate act of giving back to God what you might have claimed for yourself.[5] Both resting and tithing test your belief in God's provision. According to an old Reformed confession, refusal to rest indicates that you "have not sought first the kingdom of God and His righteousness (Matt. 6:33), but wealth, worldly cares, [and] work in the fields, to the neglect of" listening to God.[6] The Sabbath principle safeguards against basing a life on productive effort to the neglect of a trusting walk with the Creator.

Your rest is not a work by which you engender God's favor. It is quite literally the opposite of a work. We who "labour and are heavy laden" stop from our striving and receive the rest Jesus promises to give (Matt. 11:28–30). Before you take on a career, understand the beauty of rest and commit to receiving the rest God wants for you.

Like all theology, a theology of rest must be lived out; it must become woven into the fabric of your life.

You Need a Rhythm of Rest

In its most basic application, the fourth commandment calls even hard workers to habitually focus on other matters that are vital for a rich life with God.

You Need Weekly Rest

For most workers on most weeks, true rest demands putting a full stop to regular work every seventh day. But a biblical theology of Sabbath—literally *rest*—does not argue for inactivity. The Lord's day calls for a different kind of vocational faithfulness. On Sunday God wants "all those other works which men ordinarily perform on the other days of the week...[to] give place to the private and public worship of God."[7] The day itself teaches us that we must rest and that we are called to sanctify, or honor, that rest through holy activities.[8]

Aligning rest with activities may surprise us. But, as Calvin observes, "Surely God has no delight in idleness and sloth, and therefore there was no importance in the simple cessation of the labours of [the Israelites'] hands and feet."[9] You can actually profane the Lord's day, and miss the rest God wants for you, through laziness![10] Truly those who "devote themselves to a scrupulous and absolute cessation from all work" have not necessarily kept the Sabbath.[11] Lord's day labors of necessity, mercy, and worship demand real work!

The Lord's day's central rest-responsibility is congregational worship. God's will for me in the fourth commandment is "that I, especially on the day of rest, diligently attend church" (see Lev. 23:3).[12] Lest your worldly vocations swallow your spiritual devotion, you need one day in seven to refocus on God.[13] You violate the Sabbath when you allow yourself "to be ensnared by an insignificant excuse, from hearing and learning with longing hearts, the word of God in the company of the faithful."[14] So reject every "insignificant excuse!" Hear Kevin DeYoung's testimony:

I have never had trouble finding time for our Sunday worship services. Not once. I'm never double-booked during those times. I never feel pressure to say yes to another request or squeeze in another appointment at 11 o'clock Sunday morning. Why? Because it's a habit, has been my whole life. I go to church on Sunday. It's there. It's fixed. I've planned for it.[15]

Even during busy times God demands rest (Ex. 34:21). But God isn't only concerned about your weekly rest.

You Need Daily Rest

Solomon speaks of the vanity of rising up early and going to bed late, "eating the bread of anxious toil" (Ps. 127:2 ESV). A healthy delineation of work and rest will look different for everyone. But you cannot cheat the necessity of sleep, and there is wisdom in knowing when to step away from work to give time to other worthy pursuits. Some days will allow for little rest. Good workers recognize that and rise to the challenges, sometimes for days on end. But long-term flourishing requires proper balance. Once, following an especially rigorous period of work, Jesus told his disciples to take a break: "'Come away by yourselves to a desolate place and rest awhile.' For many were coming and going, and they had no leisure even to eat" (Mark 6:31 ESV). In some ways this should happen every day. As we prepare to sleep we can pray, "Lord of our labor, now be Lord of our rest."[16]

Cal Newport suggests three reasons why, as much as possible, you should "shut down work thinking completely" at the end of a workday: "downtime aids insights," it "helps recharge" and recover "the energy needed to work deeply," and "the work that evening downtime replaces is usually not that important."[17] His straightforward encouragement is this: "When you work, work hard. When you're done, be done."[18] At the very least, you need to set boundaries to the time and value you assign to your career.

A well-regulated work-rest balance is the biblical alternative to retirement as the culmination of our labors. Tom Nelson argues that "the common notion of a long, leisurely, and self-indulgent retirement is not something Scripture endorses, and in many ways it reflects the distortion of slothfulness."[19] Better to pace yourself so that you can work well all the days of your life in ways appropriate to your age, strength, and season of life. In that way, retirement won't mark the end of your productive activity but a suitable change of pace in your work for God.

You Need Quality Rest

It may sound obvious, but it must be said: rest is designed to be refreshing. It should invigorate and stimulate you. And even your rest must help you fulfill your highest calling, "to glorify God, and to enjoy him forever."[20] Faith sees "leisure as the period of changed rhythm that [refreshes] us for the delightful purpose of getting on with our work."[21] You are responsible to God even for how you recreate.

Without a biblical view of leisure you will gain little satisfaction from your downtime. Most of us have "seen the quality of [our] leisure time remain degraded, consisting primarily of a blur of distracted clicks on least-common-denominator digital entertainment."[22] Do not equate mere entertainment with refreshing leisure. Overconsumption of social media actually threatens high-quality leisure. It also doesn't rejuvenate us. It makes us angry, anxious, biased, distant, distracted, gullible, indecisive, and shallow. But tragically, "once you're wired for distraction, you crave it."[23] The true thinker desires not to escape the drudgery of his labors by retreating mindlessly into entertainment. Instead, he uses his off time *thoughtfully*.[24]

But how can we educate our leisure to make it more profitable?

Plan Your Rest

Today, perhaps unknowingly, you are confronted by well-funded players in a so-called attention economy; media companies are employing powerful tools to cash in on your screen time. This means you need to be strategic in your pursuit of quality rest and also resist the temptation to "default to whatever catches your attention at the moment."[25] The cost is too high; "our brains...construct our worldview based on what we pay attention to."[26] Or as Paul writes, by careless neglect of how we steward our minds, we are in danger of becoming "conformed to this world" (Rom. 12:2). You should reject entertainment that does not offer worthwhile reward. In rest, as in work, you must develop "the discipline of refusal."[27] In other words, decide in advance how you will spend your leisure time and say no to low-grade alternatives. John Stott puts it this way: "We need to develop more opportunities for creative leisure, for this is an authentic form of 'work' (even if unpaid) and a welcome relief from interminable hours of destructive television viewing."[28] Stott wrote these words a generation before the television became portable and personalized in the form of smart phones and social media.

Work at Your Rest

Paul Helm observes that "the non-Christian attitude is to see leisure in sharp contrast to work, as a period of complete inactivity and self-indulgence."[29] But in the Christian worldview a worklike element will transform even your leisure. God is always working (John 5:17), though not always in the same way (Ex. 20:11). Likewise, even in your leisure you should be striving for genuine improvement, say in your health and family relations by way of a vacation or in your knowledge through reading a good book.

Get Alone

We are suffering from a new and unhealthy condition called "solitude deprivation: A state in which you spend close to zero time alone with your own thoughts and free from input from other minds."[30] And sitting alone with your phone is not the cure but part of the problem. One way to get alone is to get outside. Strangely, researchers must now recommend "forest therapy," and doctors are writing "nature prescriptions" for those cooped up "in concrete jungles and screen-mediated virtual worlds."[31] Part of your calling, your life of faithfulness to Jesus, is to "consider the lilies of the field" (Matt. 6:28), believing that "all the beauty to be found throughout the whole creation, is but the reflection of the diffused beams of the Being who hath an infinite fullness of brightness and glory," as theologian Jonathan Edwards puts it.[32]

Use Your Hands

For some it is easy and obvious: in rest, you should use your hands. But too many of us live in a world divorced from creative and tangible work that reflects the work of God's hands. Handcrafting, even recreationally, "is an essential means by which we fulfill our human calling or vocation" and a biblical "sign of wisdom."[33] John Stott offers numerous examples of "creative leisure," most requiring hands-on activity:

> Do-it yourself improvements to the home, servicing your own car, working with wood or metal, dressmaking, pottery, painting, sculpting or writing, and community service like prison visiting and sick visiting, working with mentally or physically handicapped, [and] teaching illiterates to read.[34]

Your activity on the Lord's day will differ from your actions on weekdays. But surely some of the quality leisure activities just mentioned would improve Lord's day rest in addition to midweek rest.[35] On the Lord's day Jesus took walks with his disciples (Luke 6:1), authorized the preparation of food (vv. 3–4), and performed good works (v. 9). Reformed Scholastic Francis Turretin warns against a "Judaical precision" in Sabbath keeping by refusing to travel or engage in "innocent relaxation of the mind and body" and "diversion," some of the very things the Lord's day allows us to do.[36] His caution is especially on-point when it comes to service opportunities.

The fourth commandment calls us to balance our lives in submission to God's wisdom. In our fallen state we typically work too much or too little. The Lord's day calls us to guard against both. The math is simple: "There must be times when I won't work; otherwise I won't rest." And the theology, while humbling, is real. "I'm not so important in God's universe that I can't afford to rest. But my God-given limitations are so real that I can't afford not to."[37]

Your work is important. But it isn't the most important work. The Father created and sustains all things. The Son fulfilled the righteous requirements of the law for elect lawbreakers, fully paid the penalty that our sin deserved, currently intercedes for our salvation, and will come again in glory to redeem God's children. The Spirit convicts us of our sin, compels faith in Christ, and encourages us in everyday faithfulness. In your work you must not lose sight of God's work. And to do that well you must rest.

Steve ►►► *Program Manager*

Steve works for the General Services Administration (GSA). The majority of his work is related to construction in federal buildings and lease locations that house federal agencies.

This was not the field Steve anticipated entering when he was younger. His college major was in manufacturing and mechanical engineering. "However," he says, "I quickly figured out that was not the direction I wanted to go. It was boring."

Steve had worked in construction in high school and liked building things. So he took a year off from college to figure out what he wanted to do. He got a job pouring concrete. He eventually started his own business. This taught him the "administrative and financial side of construction." Steve's service in the United States Marine Corps taught him about teamwork and the leadership qualities necessary to properly influence people.

The federal sector is a difficult place for a Christian to work. Before he took the job at the GSA, Steve and his wife discussed the Christian's need to confess Christ publicly: "We both knew and agreed that our faith needed to direct both of our callings and not vice versa. Having as our chief end to glorify and enjoy God forever helps to eliminate the fear of repercussions of confessing Christ at work."

Steve believes that the best way he can share his faith is by how he does his work. He is also open with his coworkers about how he spends his weekends, namely by worshiping with God's people on the Lord's day. This openness has led to deep conversations.

For Steve, it isn't "necessary to love what you do. But it is critical to honor God in the place where he has you."

MANAGE MONEY WISELY

M anaging money is an important topic for anyone serious about vocational faithfulness. After all, much of the work we do earns wages. And the Bible tells us that making money is a primary and honorable reason for working (1 Tim. 5:18). We can't truly honor God in our vocations unless we investigate the financial side of work. Put simply, you need to have a biblical understanding of money and know how to use it Christianly.

Literally thousands of Scripture verses deal with money and possessions. And even if money was never specifically mentioned in Scripture, it would still be part of the estate you are called to steward for God. For this reason your money management is a reliable indicator of the state of your heart (Matt. 6:21). And poor stewardship always brings grief. Indebtedness causes stress and limits your generosity. Financial disagreements contribute to relational breakdowns. Poverty invites unethical behavior (Prov. 30:8–9). Near the start of your working years you need to develop a biblical attitude toward money and the accumulation of wealth.

In Ephesians 4:28 Paul gives financial instructions—not as an economist, but as a pastor—teaching believers how to "walk worthy of the calling with which [they] have been called" (v. 1 ESV).

Paul addresses both sides of a financial ledger, earning (through our work) and spending (to help others). How you earn and spend is a matter of faith and obedience. To understand that requires a biblical understanding of wealth.

How Should I Think about Wealth?

Everyone approaches the topic of money with a bias; some view it as a vice to be avoided, others as the answer to life's problems. A character in the musical *Fiddler on the Roof* calls money the world's curse. To this, the main character responds, "May the Lord smite me with it. And may I never recover!"[1] Both of those attitudes need to be nuanced by Scripture. Money is neither a curse nor a cure. Instead, money is a tool. It is a portable means of exchange. It has an assigned value that grants spenders access to goods and services.

Clearly money is a unique tool. Money represents vast potential to make a life based on our strongest desires. Enough money makes many materialistic dreams a possibility. Because of this, money has a way of tempting us to think about all of life materially. We can come to believe that nearly anything can be bought. So, money is "an active agent with decisive spiritual power." It "is never neutral. It is a power *before* we use it, not simply as we use it whether we use it well or badly."[2] This means that money has the potential to be either a great virtue or a terrible vice. Accordingly, we must neither idolize the accumulation of wealth nor reject proper financial ambition.

The Virtue of Wealth

Sometimes wealth is seen as an accidental byproduct of work, as if only greedy people work to get paid. And of course, "our work is about more than financial remuneration, making a profit...or career advancement."[3] Still, well-earned financial profit is inherently good. Surely wealth is preferable to poverty, as flourishing is better than languishing. Economist and investment manager David Bahnsen points out what should be obvious: "Wealthy societies build, grow, develop, cultivate, and steward. Poor societies do not."[4] If it weren't for how people wrongly gain and manage wealth, everyone would see wealth as a virtue.

It has been suggested that "Holy Scripture is not favorable toward wealth."[5] But this position squares poorly with the Bible's testimony. God is the giver of both wealth and its proper enjoyment (Prov. 10:22). Especially in the Old Testament wealth was a sign of God's favor (1 Kings 3:13). And while the New Testament issues stronger warnings against riches, it also presents ways for rich people to please God and provides numerous examples of such piety in action (see 1 Tim 6:18–19; John 19:38–39; Luke 19:1–10; Acts 4:34–37). Much good has been done in the world through the wealth building and philanthropy of godly people. Profit is both a sign of good work (Prov. 21:5) and a truly good thing.

The Reformed confessions warn against ungodly gain. But they also recognize the virtue of pursuing wealth.[6] According to the Westminster Shorter Catechism, the eighth commandment (against stealing) actually requires "the lawful procuring and furthering the wealth and outwards estate of ourselves and others."[7] To "help the poor in their need," in the words of the Heidelberg Catechism, requires not only that you "labor faithfully," but that by your labors you accumulate assets that you can put to work in the lives of others.[8] You should work to gain wealth to steward for God's glory. And if, over time, God sends you abundance, you should receive it gladly.

The Danger of Wealth

As with other powers, the potential of wealth is mixed—like fire it can warm a home or burn it down. The love of money can imperil our salvation by dominating our interests (Luke 18:22–23). It can breed haughtiness and God-forgetfulness (Deut. 8:17–18; 1 Tim. 6:17).

Wealth's risks have obvious implications for pursuing a calling. Reflecting on Jesus' statement that the gate to heaven is narrow (Matt. 7:14), William Perkins writes, "Now, when in the works of our calling, we intend only to get wealth, we...set bars on heaven's gates, and load ourselves with burdens, which make us unable to pass."[9] When Jesus warned about the difficulty of the rich entering the kingdom of heaven, the disciples were "exceedingly amazed" (19:25). They caught Jesus' sincere urgency (vv. 23–27). It is possible to be more ambitious gaining wealth than following Jesus. So William Perkins warned that it is unlawful to desire work with "a vain or greedy mind...or for lucre's sake."[10] A vocation is far more than exchanging labor for a paycheck (see Prov. 23:4–5).

John Calvin offers a simple alternative to both the outright rejection of wealth and the love of money: "We ought to use its good things in so far as they help rather than hinder our course."[11] This is the point of Jesus' odd parable about the unjust steward who reduced the debts owed to his master in order to gain friends who would care for him after he lost his job (Luke 16:1–8). Jesus isn't telling you to be dishonest but to use wealth to store up treasure in heaven (v. 9). "You cannot serve God and money" (v. 13 ESV). But you can serve God *with* your money. "The earth is the LORD's, and the fulness thereof" (Ps. 24:1); you are only his steward. You must manage money for the sake of God's kingdom, making his resources work for his glory. Unfortunately, this is not always our outlook. Paul Helm's observation is convicting:

> Our words say that we believe riches to be vanity and emptiness. Our acts seem to say that we love and seek them as intensely as those do who make them their all and their god. We say in words that 'we have here no continuing city', but in act are as eager to adorn our dwellings here as though they were our only home.[12]

For this reason, the Puritans advocated "loving the world with 'weaned affections'"; Christians may have a positive view of money while remaining immune to its charm.[13] Believers "use this world, as not abusing it" (1 Cor. 7:31). In other words, for the Christian, vocation and its rewards are "not the thing his heart is set upon," as Puritan John Cotton put it.[14]

The believer recognizes that God is greater than the gifts he gives. This attitude encourages thankfulness. From a human perspective good work deserves compensation (1 Tim. 5:18). But from a spiritual outlook, every good thing a believer possesses is the fruit of God's undeserved generosity. "What do you have that you did not receive?" (1 Cor. 4:7 ESV). You may not always want to believe it, but it's true, as Puritan John Flavel writes, "The success of your callings and earthly employments is by divine blessing, not human diligence alone" (see Deut. 8:19).[15]

How Should I Practice a Biblical Theology of Wealth?

Understanding money as a trust—an endowment given *by* God, to be managed *for* God—can help simplify your responsibility as a steward. Handling money wisely requires honorable choices in two main arenas: earning and spending. These two categories correspond to two questions: How should I acquire money? And what should I do with it? The following principles move from the first question to the second.

Earning Promotes Human Flourishing

In Ephesians 4 Paul sketches some of the contours of the redeemed life. Putting on the new self enables you to honor the great commandment to love your neighbor. What does this look like in the arena of personal finance?

Consider this model: Love requires sharing. And sharing is usually impractical without capital; good intentions and well-wishes are of little use (see James 2:16). But diligent work blessed by God gives us "something to share with anyone in need" (Eph. 4:28 ESV). The acquisition of wealth harmonizes with God's purposes when it alleviates want and makes life more pleasant for both ourselves and others.[16] The Reformed marriage form puts it beautifully: "Labor diligently and faithfully in the calling wherein God has set you, that you may maintain your household honestly, and likewise have something to give to the poor."[17]

Lawful earning is a serious matter. In 1 Timothy 5:8 Paul says, "But if any provide not for his own, and specially for those of his own house, he hath denied the faith and is worse than an infidel." Failing to provide for your family is as serious as denying the gospel and rejecting God's free grace.

Fiscal fidelity looks different from family to family. Some believers cannot work due to severe limitations.[18] Still, ordinarily, the acquisition and stewardship of wealth can help "you look not only to [your] own interests, but also to the interests of others" (Phil. 2:4 ESV).

Debt Can Threaten Financial Freedom

One of the most common but unhelpful ways people acquire spending power is by borrowing. Not coincidentally, just when you start spending more independently of your parents, the opportunity for indebtedness becomes a real temptation. You are a prime target of people who sell credit cards, vehicles on payment plans, and student loans. Scripture does not fully forbid indebtedness (see Ex. 22:14; Matt. 5:42). Some borrowing is nearly unavoidable in today's economy. And a shrewd businessperson might borrow capital to gain a greater future return.

But the bad kind of debt—borrowing simply to live beyond your means—is a sign of discontent and impatience. It is this kind of debt that Scripture scorns: "The rich rules over the poor, and the borrower is the slave of the lender" (Prov. 22:7 ESV). What you borrow—the principle of the loan—will need to be repaid along with interest. So, a $5,000 used car on a five-year payment schedule at 6 percent interest will end up costing you nearly $6,000. Credit card interest rates are much higher.

Borrowing often enslaves us more than we realize. For those in debt the balance becomes harder to pay, and unexpected expenditures become crises. And debt has other hidden costs. It can inspire overworking to simply make payments. It can severely hinder generosity. And it is stressful and even dangerous. From pastoral experience Tom Nelson can write, "The ongoing daily pressure of being financially overextended by a consumptive life-style is a recipe for a host of stress-related physical maladies and has a detrimental effect on our spiritual formation as well as our interpersonal relationships."[19]

Dumping debt isn't easy—it is far wiser to avoid it in the first place. But if you are in debt, the formula is as simple as ABCD: *accumulate* no new debt, *bring* in additional income, *change* your spending habits, and *develop* a plan to pay off your debt one cred-itor at a time.

Tithing Demonstrates Faithfulness and Trust

A tithe is a tenth; in economic terms it is a tenth of one's income. Although the tithe is the baseline standard for fiscal gratitude among God's Old Testament people, it predates the ceremonial laws (Gen. 14:17–20; 28:20–22). We therefore shouldn't assume it has been abolished by the coming of Christ. And the basic needs that the tithe fulfilled—helping the poor (see Deut. 14:28, 29; Gal. 2:10) and maintaining the gospel ministry (see Num. 18:21; Luke 10:7)—are ongoing. Paul expected all wage-earners to help meet the saints' needs: "Upon the first day of the week, let every one of you lay by him in store, as God hath prospered him" (1 Cor. 16:2).

If a literal tithe—the required donation of a tenth of one's pro-duce to support the work of the Levites—is not a New Testament rule, something like it is a scriptural expectation and was the plain practice of Christians living at the time of the apostles (see Acts 6:1–4 on the distribution of the church's resources to the believ-ing widows; 2 Cor. 9:5). Comparing these early Christians' attitude toward giving with that of our own, one pastor admonishes us: Christians living in the modern era would not want to find our-selves "in a position of giving away less of our income than those who had so much less of an understanding of what God did to save them."[20] But like every metric for faithfulness, it is unhelpful to focus on the tithe's legality. Believers should give as if not required to, as if it was our own idea flowing from hearts warmed by God's grace. God loves "a *cheerful* giver" (2 Cor. 9:7, emphasis added), one who finds true joy giving to the Lord.

You should start tithing now. It won't get easier as your earning power and responsibilities increase. And if you believe that it is truly better "to give than to receive" (Acts 20:35), delay in giving is a waste.

Thrift Can Ease Financial Pressure

There is no strict rule for how people should spend their money; Calvin notes that "this freedom is...to be left to every man's conscience to use as far as seems lawful to him."[21] But Scripture does require moderation, what could also be called thrift or frugality. God forbids in his stewards "all...useless waste of his gifts," according to the Heidelberg Catechism.[22] Herman Bavinck wrote that wastefulness is one of the chief vices of stewards.[23] Truly, "a foolish man devours" his resources (Prov. 21:20). Instead of pacing himself he eats and drinks whatever is at hand and thereby comes to poverty (23:20–21).

By contrast, thriftiness employs the biblical virtue of delayed gratification, making temporary sacrifices to gain a richer return (Mark 10:28–31). Admittedly, frugality can easily turn into selfishness and greed. A miser knows he should be generous, and sometimes seems to be, but his heart hates to see his savings decrease (Prov. 23:7). It is good to save money, but not by always waiting until someone else offers to pick up your lunch tab.

Still, thoughtful, biblical thrift is a virtue. It can reduce your onerous workload, compared to peers who must take all the overtime possible in order to meet unnecessary payments. It can aid generosity—in simple terms, if you eat the whole bag of popcorn, you won't have any to share. It can reduce the stress that comes from wondering if there will be enough money left at the end of the month.

Thriftiness can also facilitate the practice of investing. A teenager who saves and then invests $25 a month—less than a coffee a week—will invest nearly $15,000 of his own money over a period of fifty years; but that amount will turn into nearly $100,000 at the end of that term. Thriftiness paired with investing can make a big difference. How much do you like coffee?[24]

Return on Investment [25]

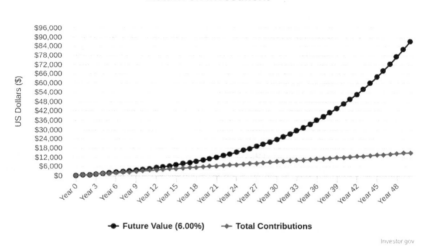

Most people find it beneficial to practice thrifty living by making a budget—an estimate, usually at the beginning of the month or a pay period—of projected income and expenses. Having a budget in place can reveal spending habits that are less easily seen through uncalculated financial activity. Ideally, you will learn to cut or reduce a line in the budget if funds are needed for a more important cause elsewhere; entertainment costs, for example, can go a long way toward paying Christian education expenses. And you don't have to budget alone. Church deacons can help evaluate your budget and offer suggestions for more prudent stewardship.

Saving and Investing Help You Prepare for Tomorrow

Now—especially while you are young—is the time to save and invest. Unfortunately, most people don't. Many Americans would struggle to pay for a $400 emergency.[26] They have little stored-up capital. God tells us to look to the wisdom of the ant: "Ants are creatures of little strength, yet they store up their food in the summer" (Prov. 30:25 NIV). And unlike the ant's food stores, in modern economies investments can grow over time through the power of such realities as compound interest and growing stock dividends and multiple expansions. (If that last sentence made your head spin, Jim Newheiser's book, *Money, Debt, and Finances: Critical Questions and Answers,* is a very accessible and useful guide written from a biblical perspective.[27]) What many people wish they had learned earlier, however, is that taking advantage of these tools requires time. So, start as early as possible.

Following Paul's simple personal finance outline of earning and spending to provide for yourself and your neighbor is the way we can implement a theology of wealth. But it also teaches us the glory of the gospel. Our hope rests on the earning and spending of Christ. The "ransom of [our lives] is costly"; "truly no man can ransom another" (Ps. 49:7–8 ESV). But Jesus possessed more than we could ever earn—a perfectly righteous life—so that he could spend more than we will ever know. Through his active obedience Christ earned the right to be our Savior (Heb. 5:8–9). Through his passive obedience he paid the price to purchase our lives: "Though he was rich, yet for your sakes he became poor, that ye through his poverty might be rich" (2 Cor. 8:9). Your wise handling of personal finance is meaningful because of Christ's earning and spending. And it is one of the most practical ways you can thank God for his indescribable gift (9:15).

David ►►► *Wealth Manager*

David runs a wealth management firm with sixty employees in seven offices, overseeing assets totaling about $5 billion. From a young age David aspired to work in finance. And he received frequent advice from his father, a pastor who was a deep source of godly, practical wisdom.

David is passionate about markets because of the opportunities they afford for kingdom influence. He also points out that the modern free enterprise—a market economy—allows people to work in places that match their passions and skills.

This calling is not for everyone. David says, "If I had known that about 95 percent of people who enter a career in wealth management fail, I probably wouldn't have done it. But I didn't know." And it wasn't easy. David encourages young people to prepare for vocational struggle: "What has helped most in my career are moments of adversity and distress. Most people struggle in the early stages of their career. I would encourage young people to recognize the struggle as a glorious thing. You will almost inevitably learn from it and grow from it." There is no replacement for difficulty. And "happiness really is a by-product of earned success."

The kinds of problems David faces are like those in other industries. But wealth management is uniquely subject to unpredictability: "You don't control what the markets will do; you don't control how people will respond to the market." This can be very humbling.

David wants all workers to labor not only to provide for themselves and their families, to tithe and support worthy causes, and to be able to witness for Christ in their work, but also because "making widgets, developing services, providing legal counsel, educating preschoolers, whatever the vocational calling may be, actually matters."

APPENDIX

QUESTIONS ABOUT VOCATION

WHAT IF
I HATE MY JOB?

Work is meant to be rewarding. It isn't the sum of your life. But it is good to enjoy what you do. Still, sometimes you don't. What do we do when work doesn't work?

Your impulse might be to quit. But usually you shouldn't; sometimes you can't. Need often trumps want. Hard jobs might not be your destiny, but reality sometimes requires painful perseverance. And perhaps with faithfulness, your work situation will improve. Some of the guidance you have received in this book can resolve moderate workplace unhappiness. You should continue to develop vocational gratitude, practice diligence, be content even in humbling circumstances, and expect God to provide an increase for your labors. You should keep cultivating skills that will make you more useful and hopefully better appreciated and compensated. In this broken world workplace unhappiness is normal; you shouldn't react to it with foolish impulsivity.

But sometimes what you do for work seems irredeemable. You might wonder if you can even go on. What can you do when you hate your job?

What Do You Mean by *Hate*?

Some people hate their jobs for the wrong reasons—the work is hard, not fully satisfying, doesn't offer enough hours or demands too many, and requires interaction with difficult people. It may be that resentment we feel about our work can be traced to "ingratitude, inability to accept a lowly place at the beginning...or arrogance and lack of discipline."[1] Vocational frustration may also stem from poor assumptions, jealousy, or stubbornness.

If we think we hate our work, we may need to adjust our expectations. On this side of glory work *must* disappoint. Steven Garber puts it like this:

> Whatever our vocation, it always means making peace with the proximate, with something rather than nothing—in marriage and in family, at work and at worship, at home and in the public square...That is not a cold-hearted calculus; rather it is a choice to live by hope, even when hope is hard.[2]

Os Guinness puts it simply: "To find work now that perfectly fits our callings is not a right, but a blessing."[3]

Even the apostle Paul maintained a less-than-ideal side job to support his primary calling as a gospel minister. And although Paul's main work truly fit his calling, it too was extremely hard. He talked about it like it almost killed him (2 Cor. 11:23–29); then it did. Too many people expect too much from their work. God-honoring vocational living is far different from fulfilling your childhood dreams. It isn't meant to meet all your needs; only God can do that.

You don't have to completely love your job. Deriving happiness from what you do is not your main purpose; your chief end is to glorify God and to enjoy him. You must come to work knowing who you are in Christ and looking only to him to "supply all your need according to his riches in glory" (Phil. 4:19).

Still, you can combat workplace dissatisfaction. Here are three ways.

Be Content

As we saw in chapter 7, contentment is a vocational necessity. Work is challenging. It will not be everything you want it to be. To put it differently, your work will not make you content, *you* must bring contentment to work. And if you hate your work without warrant, you are not in a good place spiritually. You must repent of your ingratitude and "let all bitterness, and wrath, and anger, and clamour, and evil speaking, be put away from you, with all malice" (Eph. 4:31).

The good news is that if you truly desire to be content with your work, like Paul, you can learn to be (Phil. 4:11). So, look for ways to rejoice in your work as God rejoices in his (Ps. 104:31). Contentment often comes through thankfully accepting divine providence. For right now, and for good reasons, God has given you the job you have.[4] This is a critical realization. Because, as Calvin writes, everyone "will bear and swallow the discomforts, vexations, weariness, and anxieties in his way of life, when he has been persuaded that the burden was laid upon him by God."[5]

Be Conscientious

Be committed to your duty no matter what. Your first (or second or third) job might not be your career. It might be a launching pad for better work. But it is still important. It is where you can learn faithfulness in small things. Teaching recently in a state prison confirmed for me the need to prioritize vocational faithfulness over compatibility. Most of the inmates were not living out their childhood dreams. They had limited work opportunities—they were students, groundskeepers, kitchen staff—and little hope of what we might consider advancement. Before incarceration one man was a successful demolition technician in the military. In his words (and for obvious reasons), "There is no application for that here. If my occupation defined me, then I am now nothing."

A craftsman whose work I admire recently admitted this about his job: "[It] is my life. It's the only thing that gives me a sense of identity." If you took it away from him, he says, "I wouldn't know who I was anymore." That's not good. Your vocation can't bear that burden of expectation. Vocation is about being faithful where God has placed you—doing the next thing and doing it well (see 1 Cor. 4:2). This is what Jesus did in his difficult, unglamorous calling as a carpenter. This was part of how he came to do God's will (Heb. 10:7). Instead of being a carpenter, he could have taken your difficult job as a dispatcher, restaurant waiter, IT intern, or parts manager, and done it with joy and excellence, in a way that pleased the Father.[6] Even after being publicly recognized as the Messiah, Jesus continued to do dirty work, touching lepers, feeding the hungry, washing feet. So can you. Faithfulness isn't flashy. It is, as Eugene Peterson puts it, "a long obedience in the same direction."[7] And, as Puritan Jeremiah Burroughs writes, "it is more obedient to submit to God in a low calling, than to submit to him in a higher calling...The greater the cross, the more obedience and submission."[8] And while faithfulness doesn't require satisfaction, it often leads to it.

Be Creative

Your work won't meet all of your deepest needs. Still, notes Paul Helm, a believer ought to seek real, if modest, "satisfaction in his work, and attempt, in the course of his employment, to discover and implement ways in which his work can be more rewarding, enjoyable, and useful for himself and others."[9] This is important—and encouraging—because most people find that "intrinsic satisfaction outweighs...pay, advancement, and recognition," the "external rewards," over which you have much less control.[10]

If you are frustrated at work, you might practice the discipline of "job crafting," or customizing your work in reasonable and rewarding ways.[11] What does this mean? First, most employers allow workers some flexibility to alter the type of work they do, the extent of the tasks they undertake, and the order in which they do their particular assignments. For example, you might volunteer for a night shift, which, compared with a day shift, often allows workers more freedom to fulfill their tasks. Or you might be able to trade tasks with other coworkers based on your interests and skills.

Second, you can often change how and with which people you interact at work. Maybe you get bogged down with email throughout the day. Perhaps you could just as efficiently replace some emails with more personal phone calls (or vice versa).

Finally, you can "modify the way you interpret the...work you are doing." You aren't just a checkout clerk at a pharmacy. You are part of an important chain of workers that brings medicine to sick people; you supply food and other conveniences that can truly improve the quality of life of your customers. If you struggle to find meaning in your work, you might ask a more experienced colleague, Why does what we do matter? When appropriate, you might also learn more about the people your role is meant to help, asking a senior-level employee questions like, How do the financial spreadsheets I prepare help you advise clients and prepare them for retirement?

In addition to whatever can be done to craft a more ideal work experience, you might also find ways to fulfill your creative interests and sense of calling outside of your working hours. And above all, believe that God helps his children in even their hardest work. Commenting on Jesus' parable of the talents, Herman Hanko reminds us that God "sustains [His servants] by His grace, enables them to do their calling, gives them strength for the day, courage for the moment, [and] grace for the trial of the hour."[12]

Most work can be improved. But not all.

Don't Do What You Hate

If your work is destroying your soul, you should ask yourself the hard question about whether it is time to leave for another position. After all, there are times to make prompt and drastic improvements in your vocation. Paul's parenthetical comment to slaves makes this point: "But if you can gain your freedom, avail yourself of the opportunity" (1 Cor. 7:21 ESV). Why? Because as

Calvin says, "liberty is not merely good, but is also more advantageous than servitude."[13] Slaves *can* honor God. But if one can please God in a calling that better reflects their design and in which they have greater control over their gifts, they should make a change. "We should clamor to be engaged in work," writes Dorothy Sayers, "that [is] worth doing, and in which we [can] take pride."[14]

Drawing from 1 Corinthians 7, Dan Doriani offers this simple formula about staying at or leaving a job: stay, unless, because. "We *stay* wherever we work, *unless* we can move to a better position in our social structure *or* improve the social structure itself, *because* God's people are responsible for themselves and for the wider world."[15]

Don't continue to do what you hate. But be sure that God would agree with your hatred.

IS MY VOCATION COMPROMISED BY SIN?

We can have serious doubts about whether current or potential work is appropriate for us to do as redeemed children of God. One friend wondered if she should continue serving on an advisory board that sometimes supports causes she can't endorse. People considering joining the armed forces might ponder how they can follow orders that seem contrary to biblical ethics. Can you work for companies that actively promote an LGBTQ+ agenda? What can discerning Christians do during Gay Pride Month when their company produces supportive ads? Is it okay to stock shelves with products that are harmful? What if a boss tells you to do something you think is wrong? These are complex questions, but Scripture can help answer them.

Don't Quit Yet

There may be good reasons to stay in a job that matches your skills, meets your desires, and ministers to others, even if that job presents moral dilemmas. For starters, remember that your work is how you serve your neighbor, not how you earn salvation. Luther's argument about ethically complicated work was this: "Christians can fulfill a vocation guilt-free because...the Christian is no longer in an ethical orientation toward God."[1] That is, believers are not in a covenant of works with God. We are not "under the law, but under grace" (Rom. 6:15). We don't have to be paralyzed by fear at the thought of coming up short despite our best intentions. We *will* fail. Only the self-deceived think they can do meaningful work without sinning (1 John 1:8). But as sinners who are also believers, we claim the powerful, cleansing blood of Christ (v. 7). Jesus frees us from the penalty of sin and delivers us from allowing the fear of failure to keep us from living boldly (Matt. 25:24–25).[2] This is not antinomianism. It would be wrong to excuse sinful thoughts, words, or actions at work "that grace may abound" (Rom. 6:1–2). But because you are no longer under the law, you can say with confidence, Even if I unwillfully make the wrong decision living out my vocation, I have no doubt that God will cover all my sin and still accept me as his beloved child. Justification by grace alone— and not by our works—can be a huge help in matters of conscience that are hard for us to clear up.

It is also worth pondering that "God set up [our] vocations in a messy world."[3] Vocation today assumes imperfection. So, in the words of Paul Helm, "there is a certain sort of flexibility that is both inevitable and acceptable to the Christian."[4] Vocational flexibility is *inevitable* because we live in a society; no man is an island able to cultivate a vocation free from the world's brokenness. Believers must have high moral expectations for themselves and for each other.

But godly living does not require us to forsake the world's institutions (1 Cor. 5:9–11). Instead, we must work in the world while striving to influence it with the principles of God's kingdom. Often that involves choosing between two defective options. For the moment you might have to pick between either working in a fast-food restaurant where some customers will overconsume unhealthy food or bagging addictive products while serving as a convenience store cashier. But choosing one of these options is not the same as deliberately charting a course to sin.

Participation in flawed and imperfect vocational contexts is also acceptable. After all, there is no other way. Vocational integrity involves laboring in the world, not answering a call to "go out of the world" (1 Cor. 5:10). And we are not responsible for the choices of others—how they may use our labor and products. Paul Helm's explanation is worth pondering at length:

> The fact that a Christian lives in a community of people limits his responsibility even though the exact boundaries of that responsibility are sometimes hard to discern. But think of what the world would be like if responsibility were not limited. The postman would have to open all the mail to see whether or not he approved of what he was carrying, the taxi-driver would have to cross-examine his fares. It would be impossible to work for a firm whose products might be used in the course of sin, or to buy goods from people who might use the profits they make in ways which are sinful. The fact that other people are responsible means that one person cannot be totally responsible for all the actual consequences of an action which he has performed...The Christian is called to do the best that he can in the total situation of which he forms a part.[5]

It is also possible to promote godliness from within even ungodly organizations. Consider two examples from Jesus' day: The Roman tax collection complex was systemically crooked, but Christians could still serve as tax collectors, honoring God by resisting the trade's inherent temptations. Roman soldiers were notorious for extorting money by threats and false accusations, but that didn't restrict the calling of soldier to unbelievers (Luke 3:12–14). Dan Doriani suggests that "believers *may* remain in compromised or even corrupt organizations, *if* they can mitigate evil there and if they are not *required* to sin."[6] Hymnwriter Henry Lyte offers this encouragement: "Take, my soul, thy full salvation, rise o'er sin and fear and care; joy to find in ev'ry station something still to do or bear."[7] That is a noble goal.

But in some instances it doesn't apply.

Some Things You Cannot Do

There are limits to Christian participation. Paul says, "Whatsoever is not of faith is sin" (Rom. 14:23). At least part of what he means is that you cannot actively violate your beliefs, even at work. William Perkins relates this dilemma to the two callings of a Christian: "The particular calling of any man is inferior to the general calling of a Christian. And when they cannot both stand together, the particular calling must give place."[8] To truly work unto the Lord means believing that even genuine human authority is never absolute (Acts 4:19–20). You are called to submit to authority. But you may not *obey* that authority, even at work, if obedience brings you to the point of committing sin. Hear John Flavel's admonition: "Do not be so intent upon your particular callings as to make them interfere with your general calling. Beware that you do not lose your God in the crowd and hurry of earthly business" (see 1 Tim. 6:9).[9] Sometimes the decision is clear; Christians "ought to obey God rather than men" (Acts 5:29). But even in less obvious matters, "Your conscience has a primary claim on your action, which supersedes your conventional social duty."[10]

Work becomes unworthy of you when it violates the fact of divine image-bearing in yourself or in those your work affects. Unworthy work is plainly counterproductive, defying God's command for man to rule over the creation (see Gen. 1:26). Contrary to the sixth commandment, unworthy work demands you to "willfully run into...danger" in the words of the Heidelberg Catechism.[11] It expects you to disrespect others or treat them unjustly, bend the truth, or engage in unethical schemes. Some work demands habitual denial of the principles of the Sabbath.[12] When the "social surround has become pathological—incomplete, archaic, willfully blind, or corrupt,"[13] Christians must be willing to say, This is no longer a place for a committed follower of Christ.

So, is it time to be done with your job? Hard, humbling work that lacks patent value is not a sure sign you should quit. Such was the work of Christ for us. And it is by his labor that Jesus gives us all *we* need to be faithful, even when work doesn't seem to work. Our Lord will give us wisdom and courage, sometimes to persevere, sometimes to say no and face the consequences. But don't forget that even though believers are under grace, you are still capable of sin on the job. Some poor work situations may be no one's fault but your own. If continuing in your current job is sinful, you must repent, which requires not only a change of heart but a change of course.

Whatever the case, God's grace is sufficient even when our work seems unworkable.

SHOULD I GO TO COLLEGE?

A frequent theme of this book is the need for young people to acquire the requisite skills for meaningful employment. That is essential. Again, "if you want a great job, you need something of great value to offer in return."[1] But there is no single path for acquiring those skills. Some will gain competency by routine, on-the-job training. Others will acquire skills and certification through an apprenticeship program or a trade school. Still others will gain degrees from liberal arts colleges. How can you know what is right for you?

I can't answer that question. But I can suggest several additional questions; answering them might help clear up your uncertainty.

What Are Your Gifts?

In previous generations no one was under the illusion that college was for everyone. Throughout history most people understood that higher education was for scholars—for those whose intellectual abilities especially fit them for a life of study or a job requiring rigorous academic preparation. That might not be you. And that's okay. You might possess the mind, body, skills, temperament, and connections perfectly suited for a rewarding trade; college might add little value to your qualifications for a great job. On the other hand, you might be optimally cut out for college. When encouraging one of my kids to go to college, I lightheartedly applied Luke 16:3, "I am not strong enough to dig, and I am ashamed to beg" (ESV). Begging was out of the question. And digging and other forms of manual labor didn't seem to be an ideal fit. Instead, his excellent high school grades and self-determination seemed to argue for a college education.

What Is Most Needed Now?

Giftedness is only one question you must ask when considering college. And though it is important, it can also be misleading. It is possible that what you are good at is, regrettably, not highly desirable in the current job market. You must consider that. If you do go to college, you should seek advice from a guidance counselor about the employment prospects for majors that interest you.

Many college graduates settle for lower-paying jobs unrelated to their course of study when they can't find work in their desired field. And yet a simple web search for "high demand jobs" in my state revealed that many sought-after workers do not need a four-year degree to secure meaningful employment. College is no guarantee of rewarding work. David Bahnsen points out that "nearly 40 percent of *non-working*, prime-age men [25–54]" in fact "*have* a college degree."[2] College doesn't work for everyone, sometimes even those who finish their studies.

What Is My Motivation for College?

For many the answer is simple: a desire for a high-paying job. But clearly money must not be the only factor when considering vocational preparation: "He who loves money will not be satisfied with money, nor he who loves wealth with his income; this also is vanity" (Eccl. 5:10 ESV). And it may no longer be assumed that college graduates earn more money. The value of a college degree has diminished in recent years. More companies are recognizing that experience can be at least as valuable as a diploma. Of course, some high-paying jobs require higher education. Those called to such a career are right to go to college toward that end.

And sometimes college may be required even when enhanced income is not the goal. If you feel called to the ministry, you will likely need to complete six to eight years of post–high school higher education. Similarly, educators—especially at Christian schools—sometimes have modest incomes. Most teachers aren't deterred by that; they teach out of a sense of mission. But to fulfill that mission requires a college education.

Try to be sure that your reasons for considering college are noble and reasonable. A college university professor shared with me this anecdote. When counseling a young man considering getting a post-graduate degree, the professor asked this question: "What is the problem to which your getting a doctorate is the solution?" That question should also be asked about an undergraduate or graduate degree.

How Do Family or Assumptions Affect Career Considerations?

As I was growing up, college was never discussed. My parents weren't anti-college, though they both finished their formal education with high school diplomas. And that was normal in the culture in which I was raised. Bottom line: I never considered college until a few years after high school graduation. Most of us grow up with implied or overt expectations regarding our future. That's not bad. But it needs to be understood. My father was a carpenter. So was I. But in my early twenties I sensed a possible call to ministry. So, I went to college. Alternately, if you are from a family of professionals, your parents may want you to follow in their footsteps, and they may need the reminder that, as a believing young adult, you are free to choose a worthy trade and forgo college entirely.

Be careful also to resist politicizing your decision about college. It simply isn't so that college is for liberals and the trades are for conservatives, or that city people go to school while country people get to work. Do not allow stereotypes to determine your future.

Can I Afford College?

This is a complex but vital question. In a very technical sense, everyone can afford college. Between scholarships and loans, actual out-of-pocket expenses are often negligible. But loans have to be paid back. And while college graduates are repaying loans, those without a degree can be saving income for a house or taking advantage of the wonder of long-term, compounding interest in their savings and investment accounts. If you must secure a student loan, treat it like medicine with serious side effects; take as little as possible, and try to be done with it quickly.

If you cannot afford college but feel you have good reasons to attend, you might consider letting the military pay for your education under the GI Bill. Unused portions of your benefits can even be transferred to eligible dependents. Military service as a means to pursue further education should not be considered, however, without weighing potential spiritual challenges and risks, something considered in the following appendix.

Is the Time Right for Me to Go to College?

I spent two and a half years between high school and college. For me this was exactly what I needed. My complete lack of academic application in high school suggested that college was not right for me, at least not immediately. I was glad to be done with school, forever, as far as I knew.

It is possible that you are not ready for college. From a spiritual perspective, moving away from structures of accountability (home, church, friends) without having formed deep habits of responsibility and morality can be dangerous. College might be exactly the wrong thing if your convictions are unformed or untested. For reasons including these, you might consider attending a local community college or four-year university (or a combination of the two) while living under your parents' roof, attending the same church, and retaining good local friends.

If you go to college, you should consider attending a Christian college, though this isn't always possible or practical.[3] Either way, John Piper offers five points of advice: go to war, love the word, invest in a church, find good friends, and ask God for help.[4] College is a battleground of ideas. And in many institutions the rules of engagement are biased against believers. So, college students must feed themselves on the word, seek accountability and equipping in friends and fellow believers, and pray that God would give them grace in their time of need.

The question about college is important. But it isn't all-important. It shouldn't make you panic. Use providence as a guide—go to college if you can and if you think you should. Or avoid college if you can and if you think you should. Get good advice. And finally heed Kevin DeYoung's counsel: "Make a decision. Don't over-spiritualize. You can serve the Lord in a thousand different jobs...You can be just about anything you want as long as you aren't lazy (Proverbs 6:6–11; 26:13–16)."[5]

IS MILITARY SERVICE A GOOD OPTION FOR ME?

An unbiased study of Scripture reveals a favorable view of the calling of soldiers. God himself is a warrior, "a man of war" (Ex. 15:3). Almost 250 times Scripture calls God "the Lord of hosts" or the Lord of armies.[1] In the Old Testament literal war against Israel's enemies was integral to God's work of redemption. In the New Testament the theme of spiritual warfare draws on the theme of military service. Paul charged Timothy to "endure hardness, as a good soldier of Jesus Christ" (2 Tim. 2:3). And soldiers, especially Gentile soldiers, are praised for their faith and their spiritual insight (Matt. 8:10; Acts 10:1–2). Proper military service is clearly compatible with a life of repentance and faith (Luke 3:8, 14) and renders true obedience to God (Rom. 13:4) and service to one's neighbor. The calling to protect is inherently Godlike. One would not like to imagine war without Christian leaders stationed throughout all ranks making critical decisions.

And military service can offer many personal benefits. It can teach the disciplines of respect, order, cooperation, and courage. It can develop practical skills like leadership and problem solving that are transferrable to civilian work. My friend Brian used to fly fighters in the Air Force; now he flies for a commercial airline.

Among other advantages military service offers good pay and benefits, the prospect of free college after discharge, and the promise of a pension and other medical benefits upon retirement. There are many good reasons to consider working in the armed forces.

But there are other factors for Christians to consider. The nature of the calling can raise daunting moral questions. When I asked Brian to speak to some of these moral challenges, he said bluntly: military service "involves killing people, destroying property, and facing life-threatening consequences on a near daily basis." These things cannot be taken lightly.

In response to these realities some people are fervently anti-military and anti-war. But pacifism fails the test of biblical scrutiny. As C.S. Lewis observed, pacifists use Jesus' teaching on turning the other cheek (Matt. 5:39) to demand the "duty of nonresistance on all men in all circumstances."[2] This is clearly unbiblical. "The author of warfare is God," who authorizes militaristic action "for the defense of the country [and] for the repulsion of unlawful warfare and notorious injury."[3] Reformed confessions affirm that when lawful authorities engage in just war, they, and the soldiers uprightly engaged in the conflict, serve God and fulfill their calling.[4] Still, war is messy. Not all war is just. Not all actions in a just war are right. And even defensible acts can create conscientious upheaval and psychological trauma.

And Christian soldiers face challenges even in peacetime. The average new recruit is young and often leaves the influences of home and church far behind. Military branches feature the typical problems associated with immaturity and folly, with an added boost of bravado. A cousin who has made a career in the army offered this caution:

> The military has many subcultures—smaller groups within the larger military community—but heavy drinking and the attitude of "work hard, play hard" are prevalent throughout...For many young military members hedonism

can become the norm, and soldiers have easy access to temptation. The areas surrounding military posts have cleaned up a lot in the last twenty years but still have a high density of bars, strip clubs, EZ money shops, and liquor stores. Many military subcultures promote sexual impurity (e.g., casual sex and pornography), and some promote marital infidelity, or at least normalize it. The enlisted cultures are at higher risk than the officer cultures.

Historically female soldiers have been exposed to greater danger of sexual assault than those in the general population. One ex-military female friend told me that consulting with a godly woman who has served in the military "would be an invaluable resource" for any woman considering military service.

Military service also challenges a Christian's commitment to meaningful church membership and participation. There are helpful Christian groups such as Navigators and Officer Christian Fellowship, and the potential for mentoring by strong Christian leaders and chaplains, though not every Christian group or mentor is equally faithful to Scripture. Thriving Christian soldiers will be intentional about choice of friends and accountability networks. Still, to "diligently attend church" on the "day of rest"[5] as the fourth commandment requires is not easy as a soldier if your assigned duty station is far from your church home and especially if you are deployed.

Christians can serve in the military. They can even thrive there while serving their country, making wise decisions, modeling Christlike behavior, and resisting the challenges of the vocation. But given the nature of the commitment, those considering the calling must be sure to ask important questions and seek clear answers, especially from serious believers who can speak from experience.

AM I CALLED
TO THE MINISTRY?

As we learned in this book, throughout much of church history only so-called "religious workers" had callings. Ordinary people simply had jobs. But Scripture tells us that all believers are, in fact, "servants of the LORD" (Ps. 113:1). Reformed pastor and professor R. B. Kuiper succinctly states the biblical position that "every living member of the body of Christ is undeniably a partaker of Christ's anointing and hence a prophet, a priest and a king."[1] Gospel ministry is but one of countless opportunities to live out the office of believer. Paul Helm explains the distinction between Christian ministry and other lawful vocations: "The difference between minister and cobbler is functional: both are equal as believers before God, both have worthwhile work, but that work is different merely because each has a different gift and opportunity."[2]

Nor does the special call to gospel ministry "restrict anyone from Christian service. All believers are called to serve the King, living life 'on the witness stand,' bearing testimony to his gospel."[3] Every believer, writes Charles Spurgeon, can and must "disseminate the gospel."[4] In the early church regular Christians spoke the gospel in Antioch so that "a great number believed, and turned unto the Lord" (Acts 11:21). There, under the influence of ordinary believers, "the disciples were called Christians first" (v. 26).

The evangelists were not ordained pastors. But they were effective because "the hand of the Lord was with them" (v. 21).

Still, there must be pastors and teachers "for the perfecting of the saints, for the work of the ministry, [and] for the edifying of the body of Christ" (Eph. 4:12). The ministry isn't better than other vocations. But for some, becoming a minister is the best work because God has called them to it.

Too often *how* God calls men to the ministry is needlessly shrouded in mystery. As a result, men give little thought to the possibility of gospel service, and believers fail to help them find their calling. If God calls ordinary Christian men to become pastors, you should know how he does it.

How Are Men Called to the Ministry?

Put simply, qualified men are sent by the church to speak for Christ (Rom. 10:14–15). That sending process will be different for every man. But the pattern we should expect is less like the dramatic and unmistakable call of the Old Testament prophets, and more like the pathway to ministry of Paul's spiritual son Timothy.[5] Timothy was raised in a godly home (2 Tim. 1:5), was converted to Christ as a young man, and developed a good reputation in the church (Acts 16:1–2). When Paul met him, he "wanted Timothy to accompany him" (v. 3 ESV). So "the council of elders laid their hands" on him to set him apart for the ministry (1 Tim. 4:14 ESV; see 2 Tim. 1:6). Even Timothy's story isn't programmatic. But it may help demystify the calling process. He had no "Damascus road experience." He was a faithful and gifted man taken from another calling to serve the church. So how do men like Timothy enter the ministry today?

Prayer

Jesus once appointed seventy-two men to preach the gospel. But he knew that many more would be needed. So he said, "The harvest truly is great, but the labourers are few: pray ye therefore the Lord of the harvest, that he would send forth labourers into his harvest"

(Luke 10:2). It is not uncommon for denominations and church networks today to have pastoral vacancy rates of 10 to 20 percent. And even churches that aren't vacant would benefit from more pastors, evangelists, and church planters. Pray that God would raise up pastors who reflect God's heart for the church (Jer. 3:15), to "plant, water, and harvest a people for [his] name."[6] If you are wondering if you might be called to the ministry, you should pray that the Lord would help you be faithful in your present responsibilities and also humbly respond to the possibility of a life of gospel ministry.

Encouragement

If there are young, godly men in a church, the Lord might be calling them to the ministry of the word and sacraments. And he might answer your prayers for gospel workers through your sincere encouragement. Pastors and elders should seek and equip faithful men whom God might use to shepherd the flock (2 Tim. 2:2),[7] testing potential future pastors long before they go to seminary. Parents also have an important role to play in the calling process. William Perkins puts it strongly: "Every Christian parent, by virtue of his general calling, is to dedicate some of his male children (as much as possible) to the service of the ministry, if they have gifts and inclination of nature for that calling."[8] Perkins's comment might sound overly ambitious. But his intention is exactly right. It isn't presumptuous for a parent to help a son think through the possibility of pastoral ministry. Without such encouragement many young men might simply shrug off as far-fetched thoughts of a pastoral calling. That certainly was my experience.

If you are wondering about a call to the ministry, it would even be appropriate to seek encouragement from those who know you well and are qualified to judge your competency.

Ordination

Ultimately no one knows if he is called to the ministry until a church officially calls him to pastor their congregation and charges him to take heed to the flock that the Holy Spirit has called him to help oversee (Acts 20:28). The internal call that a man might sense must be confirmed by a literal external call and the laying on of hands. But along the way there will likely be indicators of a man's calling to the ministry.

What Are Possible Signs to a Call to the Ministry?

In addition to understanding the calling process, a man considering the ministry—and his church—should evaluate his qualifications for ministry, many of which are traits all believers should be striving for. Pastor John Newton identified three signs of a ministerial call: desire, competency, and ordination.[9]

The Sign of Desire

Paul's first word on pastoral qualification commends a man's desire to be a pastor (1 Tim. 3:1). This desire is not a "naturalistic sense of attraction": a desire to be heard, a craving for reputation, power, or wealth.[10] But a called man will *want* to be used by God in the salvation of sinners and the strengthening of the saints. He will possess an internal yearning for the ministry. A friend in pastoral ministry explains that "you must feel that burden, that tug of the heart, that nagging, piercing prod from the Lord that he," at least perhaps, is calling you "to this holy task."[11] The internal call might not begin as strongly as that. But unlike many other vocations, the ministry requires a genuine passion for the work.

The desire for the ministry needs to be an *informed* desire; young men should talk with experienced pastors to understand the challenges and count the costs. This is especially so, given that pastoral ministry is a lifetime calling.[12]

The Sign of Competency

A man who may be called to the ministry must generally meet the biblical qualifications of a bishop or overseer (1 Tim. 3:2–7; Titus 1:6–9). God's people must see in him an imperfect but true reflection of the Good Shepherd Jesus. He must have a high view of Scripture and an eagerness to obey it. He will be wise and kind, courageous and loving, convictional and sympathetic. He should possess a great capacity for discouragement and the ability to graciously receive both just and unjust criticism. He should know his weaknesses. To do the work of the ministry he will have to be self-disciplined and self-controlled. A good pastoral candidate will be generally competent, likely to succeed in any field but especially equipped for pastoral work.

His gifts will not be fully developed—that will never happen, even in glory—but they will be developing. He need not be a genius. But he must have sufficient and growing intellectual strength to "rightly [divide] the word of truth" (2 Tim. 2:15). He need not be a natural orator. But he should be a good communicator, while being humbly earnest to get better at the craft.

To see how a man might pastor, it is essential that he have a positive history—thus "not a recent convert" (1 Tim. 3:6 ESV; see 1 Tim. 5:22). Since coming to faith in Christ, how has the man actually been serving the Lord? Is he involved in the life of the church? Is he growing in the gifts required for the ministry? It shouldn't be left to the man to answer these questions. The congregation and her leaders should weigh in to help affirm, or possibly deny, a man's sense of calling, considering, among other things, his performance in a good seminary.

The Sign of Ordination

Ministers must be sent by the church. Today, all it takes to become a "pastor" is to say it is so. But as Spurgeon wrote, "An ambassador unsent would be a laughing-stock."[13] A man truly called by God to the gospel ministry will be noticed, affirmed, equipped, supported, examined, authorized, and commissioned by the church of Jesus Christ. This means that

generally a person will carry on a normal calling, continuing in the place that God in His providence has put him, and it is when he is inwardly constrained to preach the gospel, and his gifts—his ability to handle Scripture, to preach, to give leadership—are recognized by the church, that his inward call comes to be outwardly ratified.[14]

Puritan John Arrowsmith simplified the requirements for a "lawful calling" into the gospel ministry: "ability, inclination, and separation (ordination)."[15] The process is not mysterious. But the calling, like all others, is great. No man is sufficient for these things. But God is "our sufficiency" (2 Cor. 3:5). After all, the gospel ministry is *God's* ministry. People plant and water. But God provides the growth (1 Cor. 3:6). God allows people, including ministers, to assist in the transformation of lives. But he is the Lord of the harvest. Ministers are just men through whom the merciful God cares for his people.

Knowing that, we should want him to raise up men for the job. So we pray and work, trusting that he'll do it.

NOTES

Introduction

1   David L. Bahnsen, *Full-Time: Work and the Meaning of Life* (New York: Post Hill Press, 2024), 36.

2   Bahnsen, *Full-Time*, 50.

3   Gordon T. Smith, *Your Calling Here and Now: Making Sense of Vocation* (Downers Grove, IL: InterVarsity Press, 2022), 7.

4   See Westminster Confession of Faith 9.4 in Philip Schaff, ed., *The Creeds of Christendom with a History and Critical Notes*, 6th ed., 3 vols. (New York: Harper and Row, 1931; repr., Grand Rapids, MI: Baker Books, 2007), 3:623.

5   For an excellent guide especially for children who might not be able yet to work outside of the home, see Mary Beeke's *Teach Them to Work: Building a Positive Work Ethic in Our Children* (Grand Rapids, MI: Reformation Heritage Books, 2021).

6   Sandomierz Consensus, in James T. Dennison, ed., *Reformed Confessions of the 16ᵗʰ and 17ᵗʰ Centuries in English Translation*, 4 vols. (Grand Rapids, MI: Reformation Heritage Books, 2012), 3:255.

Chapter 1

1   No. 534:1, 3, in *Trinity Psalter Hymnal* (Willow Grove, PA: Trinity Psalter Hymnal Joint Venture, 2018), 534.

2   Quoted in Leland Ryken, "'Some Kind of Life to Which We are Called of God': The Puritan Doctrine of Vocation," *Southern Baptist Journal of Theology* 22, no. 1 (2018): 47.

3   Megan DeVore's research on Augustine reveals some exceptions to this rule. For example, the way the church father "writes about work proves to be a crucial stepping-stone towards vocation. A grand vision of work does emerge in Augustine's sermons, commentaries, various theological tomes, and letters." See "'The Labors of Our Occupation': Can Augustine Offer *Any* Insight on Vocation?" *Southern Baptist Journal of Theology* 22, no. 1 (2018): 26.

4   Joel R. Beeke and Mark Jones, *A Puritan Theology: Doctrine for Life* (Grand Rapids, MI: Reformation Heritage Books, 2012), 534.

5   John Calvin, *Institutes of the Christian Religion*, ed. John T. McNeill, trans. Ford Lewis Battles, 2 vols., Library of Christian Classics 20–21 (Philadelphia: Westminster Press, 1960), 3.10.6, 1:724. Puritan Richard Steele used the same "sentry-post" image: "The Great Governor of the world hath appointed to every man his proper post and province." Quoted in Leland Ryken, *Worldly Saints: The Puritans as They Really Were* (Grand Rapids, MI: Zondervan, 1986), 26. Later still, William Wilberforce echoed this language when he wrote in his journal about his vision for the abolition of the slave trade in England. He must continue his work "or quit the post which Providence seems to have assigned me." Quoted in Os Guinness, *The Call: Finding and Fulfilling the Central Purpose of Your Life* (Nashville: Word Publishing, 1998), 29.

6   William Perkins, "A Treatise on the Vocations," in *The Works of William Perkins*, vol. 10, ed. Joseph A. Pipa and J. Stephen Yuille (Grand Rapids, MI: Reformation Heritage Books, 2020), 43.

7   Paul Helm, *The Callings: The Gospel in the World* (Carlisle, PA: Banner of Truth Trust, 1987), 65.

8   Perkins, "A Treatise on the Vocations," 58.

9   See Heidelberg Catechism Q&A 32, in Schaff, *Creeds of Christendom*, 3:318. Leland Ryken explains that "medieval monasticism did not embrace the ideal of the priesthood of all believers. The idea of a high calling worthy of the title *vocation* became limited to priests. They were the only ones who had a genuine calling." "Some Kind of Life," 46.

10 Klaas Runia, "Vocation," in *Baker's Dictionary of Christian Ethics*, ed. Carl F.H. Henry (Grand Rapids, MI: Baker, 1973), 700. Italics added. KJV has "calling" for "vocation."

11 John Calvin, *Commentary on the Epistles of Paul the Apostle to the Corinthians*, trans. William Pringle (repr., Grand Rapids, MI: Baker Book House, 1984), 248. Charles Hodge gives additional examples, saying that this use of *calling* refers not to the effectual call of the Spirit but rather has "the sense of *vocation*, as we use that word when we speak of the vocation of a mechanic or of a farmer." *1 & 2 Corinthians*, The Geneva Series of Commentaries (Carlisle, PA: Banner of Truth, 1983), 122–23.

12 Hodge, *1 & 2 Corinthians*, 123.

13 Simon J. Kistemaker, *Exposition of the First Epistle to the Corinthians*, New Testament Commentary (Grand Rapids, MI: Baker Books, 1993), 230; emphasis added.

14 *A Short Explanation of Dr. Martin Luther's Small Catechism: A Handbook of Christian Doctrine* (St. Louis: Concordia Publishing House, 1965), 25.

15 Dee Grimes, "God's Imposition: the Nature of Vocation," in Joel R. Beeke, Matthew N. Payne, and J. Stephen Yuille, eds., *Faith Working Through Love: The Theology of William Perkins* (Grand Rapids, MI: Reformation Heritage Books, 2022), 174.

16 Quoted in Ryken, "Some Kind of Life," 56.

17 John Calvin, *Commentary on a Harmony of the Evangelists, Matthew, Mark, and Luke*, trans. William Pringle (repr., Grand Rapids, MI: Baker Book House, 1984), 2:143.

18 Dan Doriani, *Work: Its Purpose, Dignity, and Transformation* (Phillipsburg, NJ: P&R Publishing, 2019), 184.

19 Guinness, *The Call*, 4.

20 Dorothy Sayers, "Why Work?," in *Letters to a Diminished Church: Passionate Arguments for the Relevance of Christian Doctrine* (Nashville: Thomas Nelson, 2004; repr., Villanova Center for Faith & Learning, 2020), 11, https://www1.villanova.edu/content/dam/villanova/mission/faith/Why%20Work%20by%20Dorothy%20Sayers.pdf.

21 Heidelberg Catechism Q&A 91, in Schaff, *Creeds of Christendom*, 3:339–40.

22 Doriani, *Work*, 67.

23 Sayers, "Why Work?," 6.

24 Calvin reiterates: "A *calling* in Scripture means a lawful mode of life." *Commentary on First Corinthians*, 247, 248.

25 Heidelberg Catechism A 91, in Schaff, *Creeds of Christendom*, 3:339–40.

26 Sayers, "Why Work?," 5.

27 Doriani, *Work*, 11.

28 Sayers, "Why Work?," 2.

29 Perkins, quoted in Beeke and Jones, *Puritan Theology*, 534.

30 Jay Y. Kim, "Vocation as Exiles," in *Faithful Exiles: Finding Hope in a Hostile World*, ed. Ivan Mesa and Elliot Clark (Austin: The Gospel Coalition, 2023), 131.

31 Doriani, *Work*, 43.

32 Elizabeth Woodson, *Embrace Your Life: How to Find Joy when the Life You Have Is Not the Life You Hoped For* (Nashville: B&H Publishing, 2022), 140.

Chapter 2

1 The standard of Christian good works, according to the Heidelberg Catechism Q&A 91, in Schaff, *Creeds of Christendom*, 3:339–40.

2 Lester De Koster, *Work: The Meaning of Your Life* (Grand Rapids, MI: Christian's Library Press, 1982), vii.

3 John R. W. Stott, "Reclaiming the Biblical Doctrine of Work," *Christianity Today*, May 4, 1979, 37.

4 Belgic Confession 1, in Schaff, *Creeds of Christendom*, 3:383–84.

5 John C. Raines, "Capital, Community and the Meaning of Work," in *Through the Eye of a Needle: Readings on Stewardship and Justice* (Grand Rapids, MI: Department of Economics and Business, Calvin College, 1984), 196.

6 Paul's word for the world's present futility suggests a lack of effectiveness. "Though it aspires, it is not able to achieve." William Hendriksen, *The Bible*

on the Life Hereafter (Grand Rapids, MI: Baker Book House, 1959), 206. In the paradise to come the redeemed will achieve, or "obtain the freedom of the glory of the children of God" (Rom. 8:21 ESV). Our vocations—centered in service to God and to our neighbor—will finally be free from the frustrations imposed by sin.

7   Tom Nelson, *Work Matters: Connecting Sunday Worship to Monday Work* (Wheaton, IL: Crossway, 2011), 75.

8   Martin Luther, "The Babylonian Captivity of the Church," in *Three Treatises* (Philadelphia: Muhlenberg Press, 1960), 202–3.

9   Douglas J. Schuurman, *Vocation: Discerning Our Callings in Life* (Grand Rapids, MI: Wm. B. Eerdmans Publishing Co., 2004), 114.

10   Ludwig Lemme, "Calling, Earthly," in *The New Schaff-Herzog Encyclopedia of Religious Knowledge*, ed. Samual Macauley Jackson, vol. 2, *Basilica–Chambers* (New York: Funk and Wagnalls Company, 1908), 351.

11   Ryken, "Some Kind of Life," 52.

12   De Koster, *Work*, 42. As John Stott explains, this command "was addressed to the voluntary, not involuntary, unemployed; it condemns laziness not redundancy." John R. W. Stott, "Creative by Creation: Our Need for Work," *Christianity Today*, June 8, 1979, 32.

13   Guinness, *The Call*, 147.

14   De Koster, *Work*, 13.

15   Mary LeBar, *How God Gives Us Bread* (Cincinnati: Standard Publishing Company, 1979).

16   Perkins, "A Treatise on the Vocations," 58.

17   Guinness, *The Call*, 166–67; emphasis added.

18   Kim, "Vocation as Exiles," 137–38.

19   Michael Berg, *Vocation: The Setting for Human Flourishing* (Irvine, CA: 1517 Publishing, 2020), 73.

20   We can pray like this: "Even as we face our ordinary tasks this day, recall to our hearts the extraordinary comfort of Your promise. Grant also, we pray, the strength of Your Spirit to live out the callings You have given to us and all people as creatures made in Your image. Make us fit vessels for Your work in this world this day—a sacrifice of thanksgiving, well pleasing in Your sight and a light that shines before our neighbors." "Morning Prayer," in *Liturgical Forms and Prayers of the United Reformed Churches in North America* (Wellandport, ON: The United Reformed Churches in North America, 2018), 115.

21   De Koster, *Work*, 17.

22   De Koster, *Work*, 36.

23   E.W. Hengstenberg, *Commentary on Ecclesiastes with Other Treatises*, Clark's Foreign Theological Library 3, vol. 6 (Edinburgh: T&T Clark, 1860), 65–66.

Chapter 3

1 Calvin, *Institutes*, 2.2.15, 1:274.
2 Calvin, *Institutes*, 2.2.16, 1:275.
3 Calvin, *Institutes*, 2.2.17, 1:277.
4 Perkins, "A Treatise on the Vocations," 78; emphasis added.
5 Perkins, "A Treatise on the Vocations," 57.
6 Nelson, *Work Matters*, 58.
7 Berg, *Vocation*, 4.
8 Berg, *Vocation*, 34.
9 Oswald Chambers, "January 18: It is the Lord!," in *My Utmost for His Highest* (Grand Rapids, MI: Our Daily Bread Publishing, 1927; repr., 2020), 30.
10 Schuurman, *Vocation*, 58.
11 Schuurman, *Vocation*, 59.
12 John Flavel, *The Mystery of Providence* (Carlisle, PA: Banner of Truth Trust, 1985), 76.
13 Heidelberg Catechism A 1, in Schaff, *Creeds of Christendom*, 3:307–308.
14 Heidelberg Catechism A 2, in Schaff, *Creeds of Christendom*, 3:308.
15 Martin Luther, "The Freedom of a Christian," in *Three Treatises* (Philadelphia: Muhlenberg Press, 1960), 295.
16 Schuurman, *Vocation*, 64.
17 Luther's Small Catechism, A 170, 129. William Perkins offers a similar definition: "A good work, is a work commanded of God, and done by a man regenerate in faith, for the glory of God in man's good." William Perkins, "A Godly and Learned Exposition of Christ's Sermon in the Mount," in *The Works of William Perkins*, vol. 1, ed. Joseph A. Pipa and J. Stephen Yuille (Grand Rapids, MI: Reformation Heritage Books, 2020), 233.
18 Heidelberg Catechism A 5, in Schaff, *Creeds of Christendom*, 3:309.
19 Berg, *Vocation*, 66.
20 J.C. Ryle, *Expository Thoughts on the Gospels: Matthew–Mark* (Grand Rapids, MI: Zondervan Publishing House, 1951), 256.
21 N. T. Wright, *Surprised by Hope: Rethinking Heaven, the Resurrection, and the Mission of the Church* (New York: HarperOne, 2008), 5, 56.
22 Herman Hoeksema, *Reformed Dogmatics*, 2nd ed. (Grandville, MI: Reformed Free Publishing Association, 2005), 2:125.
23 John Murray, *Redemption Accomplished and Applied* (Grand Rapids, MI: Wm. B. Eerdmans Publishing Company, 1955), 149.
24 Westminster Confession of Faith 32, in Schaff, *Creeds of Christendom*, 3:670.
25 Belgic Confession 37, in Schaff, *Creeds of Christendom*, 3:435–36.
26 Berg, *Vocation*, 59.
27 Paul Helm, *The Callings*, 39, 134, 69.
28 Guinness, *The Call*, 31.

NOTES

Chapter 4

1. Cal Newport, *So Good They Can't Ignore You: Why Skills Trump Passion in the Quest for Work You Love* (London: Piatkus, 2016), xix.
2. Herman Bavinck, *Reformed Dogmatics*, vol. 2, *God and Creation*, ed. John Bolt, trans. John Vriend (Grand Rapids, MI: Baker Academic, 2004), 203.
3. Mark Noll, *The Scandal of the Evangelical Mind* (Grand Rapids, MI: Wm. B. Eerdmans Publishing Co., 1994), 253.
4. Os Guinness, *Fit Bodies, Fat Minds: Why Evangelicals Don't Think and What to Do about It* (Grand Rapids, MI: Hourglass Books, 1994), 141.
5. Cal Newport, *Deep Work: Rules for Focused Success in a Distracted World* (New York: Grand Central Publishing, 2016), 159.
6. Iris Murdoch, quoted in Steven Garber, *Visions of Vocation: Common Grace for the Common Good* (Downers Grove, IL: InterVarsity Press, 2014), 169.
7. As William Perkins puts it, "If you would lead a life unblameable both before God and man, you must first of all bethink yourself what is your particular calling, and then proceed to practice the duties of the moral law, and all other duties of Christianity in that very calling." "A Treatise on the Vocations," 59.
8. Westminster Larger Catechism A 122, "Larger Catechism," The Orthodox Presbyterian Church, https://www.opc.org/lc.html.
9. Westminster Larger Catechism Q&A 125, https://www.opc.org/lc.html.
10. Heidelberg Catechism Q&A 107, in Schaff, *Creeds of Christendom*, 3:346.
11. Westminster Larger Catechism Q&A 141, https://www.opc.org/lc.html. The reformers rejected the logic of the monastics who, like St. Benedict, could regard private ownership among monks as a "most wicked vice." Saint Benedict, *The Rule of Our Most Holy Father St. Benedict, Patriarch of Monks* (London: Pax, 1875), 151, https://tinyurl.com/2474m6qv.
12. Heidelberg Catechism Q&A 110, in Schaff, *Creeds of Christendom*, 3:347.
13. Westminster Larger Catechism Q&A 147, https://www.opc.org/lc.html.
14. Kim, "Vocation as Exiles," 133.
15. Newport, *So Good They Can't Ignore You*, 38.
16. Newport, *So Good They Can't Ignore You*, 44.
17. Sayers, "Why Work?," 8.
18. Smith, *Your Calling Here and Now*, 114.
19. Smith, *Your Calling Here and Now*, 92.
20. Anders Ericsson, cited in Cal Newport, *So Good They Can't Ignore You*, 83.
21. Alexander Maclaren, "Esther, Job, Proverbs and Ecclesiastes," in *Expositions of Holy Scripture* (Chicago: W.P. Blessing Company, n.d.), 228.
22. Maclaren, *Esther, Job, Proverbs, and Ecclesiastes*, 232.

Chapter 5

1. Smith, *Your Calling Here and Now*, 9.

144

NOTES

2   Westminster Confession of Faith 9.1, in Schaff, *Creeds of Christendom*, 3:623.

3   Lemme, "Calling, Earthly," in Jackson, *The New Schaff-Herzog Encyclopedia*, 351.

4   Heidelberg Catechism Q&A 55, in Schaff, *Creeds of Christendom*, 3:325. While this question is asked about the communion of saints, its authors surely envision Christians using their gifts in the world.

5   Smith, *Your Calling Here and Now*, 24–25.

6   Smith, *Your Calling Here and Now*, 16.

7   Booker T. Washington, *Up from Slavery: An Autobiography* (New York: Doubleday, 1901; repr., Bottom of the Hill Publishing, 2010), 32.

8   Perkins, "A Treatise on the Vocations," 62.

9   Grimes, "God's Imposition," 182.

10 Calvin, *Institutes*, 4.20.4, 2:1490. Puritan Thomas Adams agreed, calling "the government of men...the highest and busiest vocation." Quoted in Ryken, *Worldly Saints*, 174.

11 John Cotton, "Christian Calling," in *The American Puritans: Their Prose and Poetry*, ed. Perry Miller (Garden City, NY: Anchor Books, 1956), 174–75.

12 Newport, *So Good They Can't Ignore You*, 43.

13 Smith, *Your Calling Here and Now*, 113.

14 Newport, *So Good They Can't Ignore You*, 4.

15 Newport, *So Good They Can't Ignore You*, 14–18.

16 Nelson, *Work Matters*, 152–53.

17 *Ernest Hemingway: Wrestling with Life*, directed by Stephen Crisman (A&E, 1998).

18 For further insights into the wrong way to chase your dreams, see William Boekestein, "Hemingway Chased His Dreams to Their Bitter End," *The Gospel Coalition*, February 3, 2023, https://www.thegospelcoalition.org/article/hemingway-chased-dreams-bitter.

19 Calvin, *Institutes*, 3.7.1, 1:690.

20 John Calvin, *Commentaries on the First Book of Moses Called Genesis*, trans. John King (repr., Grand Rapids, MI: Baker Book House, 1989), 1:217.

21 Calvin, *Commentaries on the First Book of Moses Called Genesis*, 1:218.

22 Doriani, *Work*, 95–96.

23 Flavel, *The Mystery of Providence*, 75.

24 William Perkins, "Commentary on Galatians," in *The Works of William Perkins*, vol. 2, ed. Paul M. Smalley (Grand Rapids, MI: Reformation Heritage Books, 2015), 52–53.

25 Schuurman, *Vocation*, 46.

26 William Perkins, "How to Live, and That Well," in *The Works of William Perkins*, ed. Joseph A. Pipa, J. Stephen Yuille (Grand Rapids, MI: Reformation Heritage Books, 2020), 16.

27 Perkins, "How to Live, and That Well," 17.

28 Helm, *The Callings*, 62.

29 Herman C. Hanko, *The Mysteries of the Kingdom: An Exposition of the Parables* (Grand Rapids, MI: Reformed Free Publishing Association, 1975), 289.

30 John Frame, *The Doctrine of the Christian Life (A Theology of Lordship)* (Phillipsburg, NJ: P&R Publishing, 2008), 312–13.

31 Schuurman, *Vocation*, 4.

Chapter 6

1 Helm, *The Callings*, 98.

2 Luther's Small Catechism, 25.

3 Gene Edward Veith Jr. and Mary J. Moerbe, *Family Vocation: God's Calling in Marriage, Parenting, and Childhood* (Wheaton, IL: Crossway, 2012), 20.

4 *Gender as Calling: The Gospel & Gender Identity* (Pittsburgh: Crown & Covenant Publications, 2017), 21.

5 *Gender as Calling*, 22, 25.

6 Nancy R. Pearcey, *The Toxic War on Masculinity: How Christianity Reconciles the Sexes* (Grand Rapids, MI: Baker Books, 2023), 31.

7 Gregg Johnson, "The Biological Basis for Gender-Specific Behavior," in John Piper and Wayne Grudem, eds., *Recovering Biblical Manhood and Womanhood* (Wheaton, IL: Crossway Books, 1991), 281.

8 Rosaria Butterfield, *Five Lies of Our Anti-Christian Age* (Wheaton, IL: Crossway, 2023), 10.

9 John Piper, "A Vision of Biblical Complementarity: Manhood and Womanhood Defined According to the Bible," in Piper and Grudem, *Recovering Biblical Manhood and Womanhood*, 36, 46.

10 Dee Jepsen, "Women in Society: The Challenge and the Call," in Piper and Grudem, *Recovering Biblical Manhood and Womanhood*, 391.

11 Jepsen, "Women in Society," in Piper and Grudem, *Recovering Biblical Manhood and Womanhood*, 389.

12 Jepsen, "Women in Society," in Piper and Grudem, *Recovering Biblical Manhood and Womanhood*, 391.

13 The next section will focus more on the vocational responsibilities and pitfalls unique to men.

14 Veith and Moerbe, *Family Vocation*, 25.

15 Calvin, *Institutes*, 2.8.55, 1:418.

16 Berg, *Vocation*, 28.

17 For more on how to obey the fifth commandment as a young adult, see William Boekestein, "Honor Your Parents, Even as You Age," *Core Christianity*, April 4, 2023, https://corechristianity.com/resources/articles/honor-your-parents-even-as-you-age.

18 Frame, *The Doctrine of the Christian Life*, 582.

19 Quoted in Schuurman, *Vocation*, 95.

20 Heidelberg Catechism A 54, in Schaff, *Creeds of Christendom*, 3:325.

21   Luther's Small Catechism Q&A 186, 136.

22   Quoted in Schuurman, *Vocation*, 35.

23   Belgic Confession 28, in Schaff, *Creeds of Christendom*, 3:418.

24   Heidelberg Catechism A 103, in Schaff, *Creeds of Christendom*, 3:345.

25   Westminster Larger Catechism A 117, https://www.opc.org/lc.html.

26   Westminster Larger Catechism A 120, https://www.opc.org/lc.html; emphasis added.

27   Westminster Larger Catechism Q&A 117, https://www.opc.org/lc.html.

28   Belgic Confession 28, in Schaff, *Creeds of Christendom*, 3:418.

29   Guinness, *The Call*, 49.

30   Helm, *The Callings*, 53.

31   Calvin, *Institutes*, 3.10.6, 1:725.

Chapter 7

1   *Barna*, s.v. "What Faith Looks Like in the Workplace," October 30, 2018, https://www.barna.com/research/faith-workplace.

2   Grimes, "God's Imposition," 176.

3   Guinness, *The Call*, 18.

4   Perkins, "A Treatise on the Vocations," 105.

5   Guinness, *The Call*, 92–93.

6   Amy L. Sherman, *Kingdom Calling: Vocational Stewardship for the Common Good* (Downer's Grove, IL: InterVarsity Press, 2011), 49.

7   Gene Edward Veith, "Vocation and Human Dignity," *Logia*, 31 no. 3 (Holy Trinity 2022), 15.

8   Richard Steele, quoted in Leland Ryken, "Some Kind of Life," 56.

9   Dorothy Sayers, quoted in Doriani, *Work*, 53.

10   Sayers, "Why Work?," 8.

11   Sayers, "Why Work?," 6.

12   Smith, *Your Calling Here and Now*, 12.

13   Newport, *Deep Work*, 117.

14   Newport, *Deep Work*, 226.

15   Greg McKeown, *Essentialism: The Disciplined Pursuit of Less* (New York: Crown Business, 2014), 48.

16   Cotton, "Christian Calling," 178.

17   McKeown, *Essentialism*, 121.

18   Kai-Fu Lee, quoted in Tony Reinke, *God, Technology, and the Christian Life* (Wheaton, IL: Crossway, 2022), 258.

19   Schuurman, *Vocation*, 29.

20   Smith, *Your Calling Here and Now*, 133.

21   Reinke, *God, Technology, and the Christian Life*, 261.

22   *The Conference Board*, "Survey: US Job Satisfaction Hits All-Time High," May 11, 2023, https://www.conference-board.org/press/job-satisfaction-hits-all -time-high.

23 Perkins, "A Treatise on the Vocations," 87.

24 Calvin, *Institutes*, 3.10.6, 1:725.

25 Perkins, "A Treatise on the Vocations," 91.

26 Doriani, *Work*, 110.

27 Doriani, *Work*, 155.

28 George Eliot, *Middlemarch*, quoted in Garber, *Visions of Vocation*, 188.

29 Berg, *Vocation*, 97.

30 Calvin, *Commentary on the Epistles to the Corinthians*, 251.

31 See Perkins, "A Treatise on the Vocations," 47.

32 Newport, *So Good They Can't Ignore You*, 19.

33 Sherman, *Kingdom Calling*, 144.

Chapter 8

1   Perkins, "A Treatise on the Vocations," 97.

2   Dick Gaffin, *Calvin and the Sabbath: The Controversy of Applying the Fourth Commandment* (Ross-shire, Great Britain: Mentor, 1998), 9.

3   Zacharias Ursinus, *Commentary on the Heidelberg Catechism*, trans. G. W. Williard (1852; repr., Phillipsburg, NJ: Presbyterian and Reformed Publishing Company), 561.

4   The primary purpose in the fourth commandment, according to Calvin, is to "represent...spiritual rest in which believers ought to lay aside their own works to allow God to work in them." *Institutes*, 2.8.28, 1:395.

5   Doriani, *Work*, 141.

6   The Hungarian *Confessio Catholica*, in Dennison, *Reformed Confessions of the 16th and 17th Centuries*, 2:642.

7   Ursinus, *Commentary on the Heidelberg Catechism*, 558.

8   William Ames, *A Sketch of the Christian's Catechism*, trans. Todd M. Rester, in Classic Reformed Theology (Grand Rapids, MI: Reformation Heritage Books, 2008), 169.

9   John Calvin, *Commentaries on the Four Last Books of Moses Arranged in a Harmony* (Grand Rapids, MI: Baker, 1989), 2:434.

10 Westminster Larger Catechism Q&A 119, https://www.opc.org/lc.html.

11 Francis Turretin, *Institutes of Elenctic Theology*, ed. James T. Dennison, trans. George Musgrave Giger (Phillipsburg, NJ: P&R Publishing, 1994), 2:100.

12 Heidelberg Catechism Q&A 103, in Schaff, *Creeds of Christendom*, 3:345. The author of the catechism reminds us that "the end or design of the commandment is the maintenance of the public worship of God in the church." Ursinus, *Commentary on the Heidelberg Catechism*, 557.

13 Calvin is right: "In order to prevent religion from either perishing or declining among us, we should diligently frequent the sacred meetings, and make use of those external aids which can promote the worship of God." *Institutes*, 2.8.34, 1:401.

14 Large Emden Catechism (1551), in Dennison, *Reformed Confessions of the 16th and 17th Centuries*, 598. See also Ursinus, *Commentary on the Heidelberg Catechism*, 568.

15 Kevin DeYoung, *Crazy Busy: A (Mercifully) Short Book about a (Really) Big Problem* (Wheaton, IL: Crossway, 2013), 98–99.

16 "Evening Prayer," in *Liturgical Forms and Prayers*, 115.

17 Newport, *Deep Work*, 144–49.

18 Newport, *Deep Work*, 154.

19 Nelson, *Work Matters*, 44.

20 Westminster Shorter Catechism Q&A 1, in Schaff, *Creeds of Christendom*, 3:676.

21 Sayers, "Why Work?," 7. Moses injects into the fourth commandment's mandated rhythm of work and rest the idea of refreshment (Ex. 31:17). What it means for God to be "refreshed" is mysterious. But even short breaks in human work prove the value of leisure for the purpose of rejuvenated labor. Perkins called recreation "a necessary means to refresh either body or mind," or both, "that we may the better do the duties which pertain unto us." "A Treatise of the Vocations," 97.

22 Newport, *Deep Work*, 211.

23 Newport, *Deep Work*, 160.

24 See Henry Zylstra, *Testament of Vision* (Grand Rapids, MI: Wm. B. Eerdmans Publishing Co., 1958), 187.

25 Newport, *Deep Work*, 212.

26 Newport, *Deep Work*, 77.

27 R. Kent Hughes, *Disciplines of a Godly Man* (Wheaton, IL: Crossway, 1991), 73.

28 Stott, "Creative by Creation: Our Need for Work," 33.

29 Helm, *The Callings*, 110.

30 Cal Newport, *Digital Minimalism: Choosing a Focused Life in a Noisy World* (New York: Portfolio/Penguin, 2019), 103.

31 Brett McCracken, *The Wisdom Pyramid: Feeding Your Soul in a Post-Truth World* (Wheaton, IL: Crossway, 2021), 107, 108.

32 Quoted in McCracken, *Wisdom Pyramid*, 132.

33 Smith, *Your Calling Here and Now*, 94, 97. See also Proverbs 31.

34 Stott, "Creative by Creation: Our Need for Work," 33.

35 Unlike the Heidelberg Catechism (1563) the Westminster catechisms identify "recreation" as a violation of the fourth commandment (e.g., WSC 60, 61). Westminster's critique of recreations must be interpreted against the backdrop of the 1618 publication of *The King's Book of Sports*, which directly contradicted the Puritans' Sabbath piety and urged participation in many recreations that explicitly violated the Lord's day's goal of granting rest. The *Book of Sports* "was a direct assault upon centuries of Christian teaching and tradition as well as an incursion against the ministry of the Word exercised

from the pulpit." Joel M. Ellis, "Rest, Wrestling, and Revolution: Anglican Establishmentarianism and the Puritan Sabbath," *Puritan Reformed Journal* 16, no.1 (January 2024): 119. It should also be noted that the word *recreation* may suggest to us activities that could be judged unsuitable on the Lord's day; utilizing a recreation facility could be an example. The word originally suggested mental or spiritual renewal, the very thing that the Lord's day is meant to facilitate.

36 Such forms of piety can impose "upon the shoulders of Christians an unbearable yoke...repugnant to Christian liberty and the gentleness of Christ and opposed to the sweetness of the covenant of grace by...tormenting the consciences of men through infinite scruples and inextricable difficulties." Turretin, *Institutes*, 2:98. For this reason it would not be wise to list here examples of such permissible activities.

37 DeYoung, *Crazy Busy*, 99.

Chapter 9

1 Sheldon Harnick, *Fiddler on the Roof,* music by Jerry Bock (New York: Sunbeam Music Corporation, 1964), 61, https://www.google.com/books/edition/Fiddler_on_the_Roof/hl771abfMqsC?hl=en&gbpv=1.

2 Guinness, *The Call*, 140.

3 Nelson, *Work Matters*, 124.

4 Bahnsen, *Full-Time*, 69.

5 Bavinck, *Reformed Ethics: The Duties of the Christian Life*, ed. John Bolt (Grand Rapids, MI: Baker Academic, 2021), 2:389. This comment by Herman Bavinck is surprisingly unnuanced given his robust scriptural and historical survey of the divine dispersal and genuine benefits of wealth.

6 "Regarding riches and the rich and noble estates, if they are pious and live as is right and use their riches and possessions well, then we do not censure them, nor do we consider these things not to be fitting for Christian people." Sandomierz Consensus, in Dennison, *Reformed Confessions of the 16th and 17th Centuries*, 3:256.

7 Westminster Shorter Catechism Q&A 74, in Schaff, *Creeds of Christendom*, 3:692.

8 Heidelberg Catechism A 111, in Schaff, *Creeds of Christendom*, 3:348.

9 Perkins, "A Treatise on the Vocations," 82.

10 Perkins, "A Treatise on the Vocations," 70.

11 Calvin, *Institutes*, 3.10.1, 1:719–20.

12 Helm, *The Callings*, 92.

13 Miller, *The American Puritans: Their Prose and Poetry*, 172.

14 Cotton, "Christian Calling," 176.

15 Flavel, *The Mystery of Providence*, 80.

16 See Bavinck, *Reformed Ethics*, 2:391.

17 Form for the Confirmation of Marriage before the Church, in *The Confessions and the Church Order of the Protestant Reformed Churches* (Grandville, MI: Protestant Reformed Churches in America, 2005), 307.

18 While it is permissible for a man to delegate breadwinning to his wife for weighty and justifiable reasons, the responsibility to "manage his household well" (1 Tim. 3:4 ESV) ultimately rests on him.

19 Nelson, *Work Matters*, 170.

20 Timothy Keller, *Counterfeit Gods: The Empty Promises of Money, Sex, and Power, and the Only Hope That Matters* (New York: Dutton, 2009), 62.

21 Calvin, *Institutes*, 3.10.1, 1:720.

22 Heidelberg Catechism A 110, in Schaff, *Creeds of Christendom*, 3:347.

23 Bavinck, *Reformed Ethics*, 2:394–95.

24 The 6 percent interest rate used in this illustration is only about half the annual rate of return over the span of the last fifty years in the American stock market. Young people, even minors with help from their parents, can set up a free brokerage account with a reputable investment firm like Fidelity, Charles Schwab, or Vanguard.

25 "Compound Interest Calculator," Investor.gov, https://www.investor.gov /financial-tools-calculators/calculators/compound-interest-calculator.

26 Neal Gabler, "The Secret Shame of Middle-Class Americans," *The Atlantic*, May 2016, https://www.theatlantic.com/magazine/archive/2016/05/my -secret-shame/476415.

27 Phillipsburg, NJ: P&R Publishing, 2021.

Appendix A

1 Jordan B. Peterson, *Beyond Order: 12 More Rules for Life* (New York: Portfolio, 2021), 154.

2 Garber, *Visions of Vocation*, 203; emphasis added.

3 Guinness, *The Call*, 51.

4 William Perkins' comment is meant to be encouraging: "Every man must judge that particular calling, in which God has placed him, to be the best of all callings for him." "A Treatise on the Vocations," 56.

5 *Institutes*, 3.10.6, 1:725. Leland Ryken offers this encouraging reminder: "If God through his arrangement of a person's life opens a door of opportunity, buttressed by endowments to perform a certain kind of work or activity, we can view this as summoning or calling a person to enter the open door." "Some Kind of Life," 60.

6 See Dallas Willard, *The Divine Conspiracy* (San Francisco: HarperSanFrancisco, 1998), 14.

7 Eugene Peterson, *A Long Obedience in the Same Direction: Discipleship in an Instant Society* (Downers Grove, IL: InterVarsity Press, 1980).

8 Jeremiah Burroughs, *The Rare Jewel of Christian Contentment* (1648; repr., Carlisle, PA: The Banner of Truth Trust, 1995), 198, 205.

9   Helm, *The Callings*, 104.
10 Guinness, *The Call*, 142.
11 See, for example, Jane E. Dutton and Amy Wrzesniewski, "What Job Crafting Looks Like," *Harvard Business Review*, March 12, 2020, https://hbr.org/2020/03/what-job-crafting-looks-like.
12 Hanko, Mysteries of the Kingdom, 293.
13 Calvin, *Commentary on the Epistles to the Corinthians*, 249.
14 Sayers, "Why Work?," 7.
15 Doriani, Work, 95.

Appendix B

1   As summarized by Berg, *Vocation*, 66.
2   This was roughly Luther's point in his strange word to his colleague Philip Melancthon to "sin boldly." See Ryan Reeves, "Did Luther Really Tell Us to 'Love God and Sin Boldly'?" *The Gospel Coalition*, April 20, 2016, https://www.thegospelcoalition.org/article/did-luther-really-tell-us-to-love-god-and-sin-boldly.
3   Berg, *Vocation*, 66.
4   Helm, *The Callings*, 119.
5   Helm, *The Callings*, 123.
6   Doriani, *Work*, 119.
7   No. 513:4, in *Trinity Psalter Hymnal*, 513.
8   Perkins, "A Treatise on the Vocations," 60.
9   Flavel, *The Mystery of Providence*, 79.
10 Peterson, *Beyond Order*, 148.
11 Heidelberg Catechism Q&A 105, in Schaff, *Creeds of Christendom*, 3:346.
12 Striving for excellence and being willing to work longer hours in undesirable shifts can often provide believers with capital that will allow them to bargain with employers toward honoring the fourth commandment.
13 Peterson, *Beyond Order*, 29.

Appendix C

1   Newport, *So Good They Can't Ignore You*, 44.
2   Bahnsen, *Full-Time*, 58; emphasis added.
3   Especially if you attend a secular college, or a Christian college that has drifted from biblical orthodoxy, you should consider reading Michael Kruger's *Surviving Religion 101: Letters to a Christian Student on Keeping the Faith in College* (Wheaton, IL: Crossway, 2021).
4   John Piper, "How to Stay Christian in College," *Desiring God*, August 16, 2017, https://www.desiringgod.org/interviews/how-to-stay-christian-in-college.
5   Kevin DeYoung, *Just Do Something: A Liberating Approach to Finding God's Will* (Chicago: Moody Publishers, 2009), 100.

NOTES

Appendix D

1 For more on this powerful phrase, see William Boekestein, "Lord of Hosts," *Tabletalk*, August 2022, https://tabletalkmagazine.com/article/2022/08/lord-of-hosts.

2 Quoted in Zach Kincaid, "Why I'm Not a Pacifist," *C.S Lewis*, June 19, 2014, https://www.cslewis.com/why-im-not-a-pacifist.

3 The Hungarian *Confessio Catholica*, in Dennison, *Reformed Confessions of the 16th and 17th Centuries*, 2:619.

4 Sandomierz Consensus, in Dennison, *Reformed Confessions of the 16th and 17th Centuries*, 3:257.

5 Heidelberg Catechism Q&A 103, in Schaff, *Creeds of Christendom*, 3:345.

Appendix E

1 R. B. Kuiper, *The Glorious Body of Christ* (Grand Rapids, MI: Wm. B. Eerdmans Co., n.d.), 131.

2 Helm, *The Callings*, 58.

3 John Sittema, *Called to Preach?: Pondering God's Commission for Your Life* (1989; repr. and rev., Dyer, IN: Mid-America Reformed Seminary, 2010), 22.

4 Charles Spurgeon, *Lectures to My Students* (Grand Rapids, MI: Zondervan, 1954), 22. Spurgeon adds that "the propagation of the gospel is left, not to a few, but to all the disciples of the Lord Jesus Christ: according to the measure of grace entrusted to him by the Holy Spirit, each man is bound to minister in his day and generation, both to the church and among unbelievers."

5 "An extraordinary, divine declaration is not an element of this *internal commission*...The *external calling* is also not extraordinary in nature." Wilhelmus á Brakel, *The Christian's Reasonable Service*, ed. Joel R. Beeke, trans. Bartel Elshout (Grand Rapids, MI: Reformation Heritage Books, 1993), 2:121, 122.

6 "Pastoral Prayer (Long)—1," in *Liturgical Forms and Prayers*, 102.

7 "Paul reminded Timothy that it fell within his ministerial duty to see that the ministry of God's word was effectively continued." Broughton Knox, quoted in Colin Marshall and Tony Payne, *The Trellis and the Vine: The Ministry Mind-Shift that Changes Everything* (Kingsford, Australia: Matthias Media, 2009), 128. Church orders in the Dutch Reformed tradition prioritize the encouragement of men for ministry. "The churches shall exert themselves, as far as necessary, that there may be students supported by them to be trained for the ministry of the Word." Church Order 19, in *Confessions and Church Order*, 387. "Competent men should be urged to study for the ministry of the Word." Church Order of the United Reformed Churches in North America, 3, https://www.urcna.org/church-order.

8 Perkins, *A Treatise on Vocations*, 51–52.

9 Cited in Spurgeon, *Lectures to My Students*, 33–35.

10 Joel Nederhood, "The Minister's Call," in *The Preacher and Preaching: Reviving the Art*, ed. Samuel T. Logan, Jr. (Phillipsburg, NJ: P&R Publishing, 1986), 35.

11 Jason Helopoulos, *The New Pastor's Handbook: Help and Encouragement for the First Years of Ministry* (Grand Rapids, MI: Baker Books, 2015), 29.

12 See Church Order 12, in *Confessions and Church Order*, 384.

13 Spurgeon, *Lectures to My Students*, 24.

14 Helm, *The Callings*, 67.

15 Quoted in Chad Van Dixhoorn, *God's Ambassadors: The Westminster Assembly and the Reformation of the English Pulpit, 1643–1653, Studies on the Westminster Assembly* (Grand Rapids, MI: Reformation Heritage Books, 2017), 109.

YOU MAY ALSO LIKE

Dating Differently: A Guide to Reformed Dating

by Joshua Engelsma

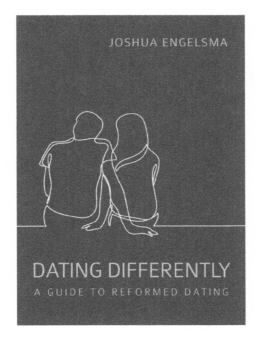

"A personal, pastoral, practical book that answers the questions dating couples will have." —*Christian Renewal*

"The author gives a trustworthy, reliable guide...for teens, their parents, teachers, and pastors." —*Clarion*

www.ingramcontent.com/pod-product-compliance
Lightning Source LLC
Chambersburg PA
CBHW020028120325
23379CB00008B/93